Mark Freeman is a mental health coach and human-centered design workshop facilitator based in Toronto. He has taught Shakespeare's plays in Korea, tended gardens in Spain, filmed an Arabic-language documentary on youth employment in Cairo, and facilitated strategy workshops for executives at multiple Fortune 500 companies. After recovering from several mental illness diagnoses, he now focuses on leveraging technology and design to help others navigate the complex changes necessary to improve and maintain great mental health and fitness. He is the co-founder of the online mental health community EVERYBODY HAS A BRAIN, and a Stanford Medicine X ePatient Scholar. His favourite pastimes include sitting and breathing.

THE MIND WORKUT

Mark Freeman

piatkus

PIATKUS

First published in Great Britain in 2017 by Piatkus

1 3 5 7 9 10 8 6 4 2

Copyright © Mark Freeman 2017

The moral right of the author has been asserted.

All rights reserved.
No part of this publication may be reproduced, stored in a
retrieval system, or transmitted in any form or by any means, without
the prior permission in writing of the publisher, nor be otherwise circulated
in any form of binding or cover other than that in which it is published
and without a similar condition including this condition
being imposed on the subsequent purchaser.

A CIP catalogue record for this book
is available from the British Library.

ISBN 978-0-349-414539

Illustrations © Mark Freeman 2017

Typeset in Sabon by M Rules
Printed and bound by CPI Group (UK) Ltd, Croydon, CR0 4YY

Papers used by Piatkus are from well-managed forests
and other responsible sources.

Piatkus
An imprint of
Little, Brown Book Group
Carmelite House
50 Victoria Embankment
London EC4Y 0DZ

An Hachette UK Company
www.hachette.co.uk

www.improvementzone.co.uk

Thank you to everybody who's tolerated my stumbling around on this journey. Thank you for offering shelter, feeding me cookies and sharing your knowledge about how to cross the rivers ahead.

CONTENTS

INTRODUCTION   1

Part One: The Basics

STEP 1
Understand that you are not a rock   19

STEP 2
Recognise your problems   27

STEP 3
Practise mindfulness   39

STEP 4
Meditate   51

STEP 5
Follow your values   65

STEP 6
Focus on changing actions, not thoughts or feelings   77

STEP 7
Stop coping   89

STEP 8
Break your IF X THEN Y thinking pattern   103

STEP 9
Stop checking   111

STEP 10
Understand your fears   125

STEP 11
Stop controlling   133

STEP 12
Tame the monster   143

Part Two: The Transformation

STEP 13
Switch the fuel for life from fear to values   155

STEP 14
Break your motivation addiction   171

STEP 15
Throw out unhelpful beliefs and desires   185

STEP 16
Practise non-judgement   199

STEP 17
Make happiness a practice   209

STEP 18
Embrace uncertainty   221

STEP 19
Plan for your wilderness adventure   231

STEP 20
Keep taking steps   243

NOTES   251

INDEX   253

INTRODUCTION

IF YOU DON'T RUN, IT'S NOT WEIRD IF YOU CAN'T RUN

This is a book about everyday actions you can take to maintain and improve your mental health. We all have varying levels of improvable mental health, and we improve mental health in the same way we improve physical fitness – by working our way through difficult experiences and developing our abilities and skills to handle those experiences.

When I say that improving your mental health is just like improving your physical fitness, I'm not suggesting that mental illnesses aren't real biological experiences. Physical fitness is all about biology.

Imagine we select a random, 30-year-old, average guy that doesn't exercise. He hasn't exercised since he left school. He says he's allergic to exercise. He hates it. But life has a way of throwing him into situations where he's forced to exert himself. Just as he arrived at his office building the other day, already a few minutes late for a meeting, the lifts broke down so he had to carry his bags up 30 flights of stairs to the office. By the third floor his heart was pounding and he was gasping for breath. He could feel the sweat soaking through his shirt.

There was no ambiguity in his mind about what he wanted to do, but no matter how much he berated himself to get up those stairs as quickly as possible, he kept stopping to catch his breath.

His muscles burned. He felt sharp pains in his knees with each step. There was no way he could hope himself into easily handling 30 flights of stairs. It wasn't a cognitive choice. He couldn't simply choose to have the strength, flexibility and endurance he needed right then. No amount of positive thinking would have given him the skills or speed to get up those stairs any faster.

Now, if we could measure the cortisol, adrenaline and blood oxygen levels in his body at that moment, we could say that he had a 'chemical imbalance'. His hormone and neurotransmitter levels would be all over the place. If we did a brain scan on him and compared that to scans of people who exercised regularly, it's likely we would see obvious differences in brain activity and structure. But none of those biological indicators would mean that he necessarily has a disease. They wouldn't indicate that he's incapable of developing the skills and physical capacity to handle that experience. We wouldn't label that guy as having an Endurance Disorder. Even if he was forced to run up the stairs every day for a week and he failed every time to do it without stopping, that still wouldn't indicate the presence of a chronic disorder. With a month or so of sweaty, difficult practice, while making changes throughout his life to support that practice, he could make that climb without stopping.

This is true with any fitness challenge. If you don't run, it's not weird if you can't run. But you can learn how to do it.

A RADICAL IDEA

I've mentioned all of this to propose something radical that we'll explore throughout this book: It's not weird to struggle with your mental health if you're not doing things regularly to maintain and improve it.

As a society, we seem to understand this concept when it comes to physical fitness. You can't take your physical fitness for granted. If you don't maintain it, you won't have it. The same is true with mental health, but for some reason we expect to be in great mental shape without doing any work or learning any skills. And when we realise we're struggling, we look for a quick and easy fix.

Currently, our society takes an illness-first approach to mental health. Help isn't available until you're lying drunk and naked in the middle of the street in a puddle of your own vomit talking to invisible monkeys. We pretend everybody who's not obviously stumbling painfully through life and failing at it doesn't have any issues with their mental health. But everybody has a brain, so everybody has mental health. I learned this the hard way …

I HAVE A BRAIN

Ten years ago, if you'd told me I'd be writing a book about overcoming mental illness and building better mental health, I would have said you were crazy. I didn't know anything about mental health, and I certainly didn't have a mental illness. But I was very wrong.

By the time I was in my late twenties, reality was increasingly something with which I struggled. Whenever I left my apartment, I'd go through a series of rituals to check the stove was off; I'd check that appliances were off, that they didn't feel hot, unplug anything I could unplug, check the windows were locked, and then, finally, leave the apartment. Then I'd lock the front door, check that the front door was locked, then debate with myself about whether my memory of checking the stove moments earlier actually came from a few moments ago or the day before. I'd leave, then go back to check that my laptop was hidden under my bed so thieves wouldn't find it, and then, realising that the curtains were open, I would close them because the thieves might have seen where I had hidden my laptop. Then I'd take it from under my bed and put it in my cupboard under some clothes before leaving the building by a different door than the one I came in by (to trick the thieves that were watching me). But then I'd have to go back to check the lock again, because I was so focused on my escape route I couldn't remember if I'd locked the front door, and since I was back at the apartment, why not check the stove again, the back door, maybe the toaster, check if there was anything near any of the plugs that could catch fire, and then jiggle the door again on the way out, then once more because the first time might have unlocked it. I'd finally peel myself away, preoccupied with imaginary conversations in my head between me and people I was upset with because of something that had almost happened the day before.

When I walked up stairs, I would see myself falling and splitting my jaw apart on the steps, teeth scattering everywhere. The bones in my face would ache like it had actually happened. When I was at a crossing, I would see cars run right over the pedestrians in front of me, splashing guts and bones across the road in front of me. I would feel like I was going to vomit.

I saw violent things happen to other people or myself all the time, and the violence was often my fault. I was afraid to carry knives in the kitchen if anybody else was around because I would see myself stabbing them. I couldn't carry a knife in the kitchen if my room-mate's cat, Glick, was there because I'd see the knife go right through Glick's head. If I was cutting vegetables I'd feel my fingers getting sliced off.

Reality was a subjective, viscerally painful experience. I developed stereotypical symptoms of Obsessive Compulsive Disorder (OCD), such as repeatedly washing my hands under scalding hot water, along with lesser-known symptoms such as checking my ID repeatedly and wondering if the person pictured on it was actually me. I was convinced I would someday hand it to a police officer and get thrown in gaol because I was impersonating somebody. This is a small selection of the extreme end of the symptoms with which I struggled. Most of the time I was just drowning in anxiety, for no particular reason. I spent all of my time and energy either ruminating or trying to find somebody to hook up with (but then not actually meeting them because of my insecurities and health anxieties).

But I didn't even think my behaviour was strange. When I first went to see a counsellor, all I told her was that I was experiencing some depression and sex issues. Those were the only problems in my life. I was very smart. I was not crazy.

Eventually, as I stumbled through the system, I had a load of mental illness labels stuck on me: OCD, Generalised Anxiety Disorder (GAD), depression and addiction. Those labels were as much about each therapist's areas of expertise as they were about what I was aware of or willing to share.

The specific symptoms I struggled with might make for great suffertainment or illness porn – everybody loves to gawk at a good car crash as they creep by on the highway of life – but, believe me that the far more interesting journey is the one of being healthy. I no longer struggle with any of those diagnoses that got stuck on me. This is not a book about my past. Nor is it a book about *having* mental illness. We'll get into some more of the symptoms I dealt with – because that will shed light on steps we can all take to improve our mental health – but if you're looking for a confessional memoir about what it's like to suffer from mental illness, this is not the book for you.

WHO IS THIS BOOK FOR?

You, your friends, your partner . . . Anybody with a brain can find value in this book because it is about practising great mental health and fitness – and everyone can improve on that. It's about learning how to experience thoughts, emotions and urges, accept them, and to keep on running into life. It's about learning how to pick up heavy emotions and carry them with you while you do the things you love with the people you love.

I've taken a journey from being very sick to being very healthy, like the mental health equivalent of somebody who goes from being dangerously out of shape to running marathons. It might have been an extreme journey but what I learned can help anyone who is interested in taking care of his or her mental health and preventing the depth of challenge that I faced.

I don't offer instant, mystical secrets to overcoming mental health challenges. Mental fitness is hard work, just like its physical counterpart. Changing your brain takes time and effort, like changing any other part of your body. I've never taken any medication for my mental health, so I don't have a perfect chemical to share or a gene for you to blame for your problems. I am not going to promote any magical supplements or special mantras. And I'm certainly not going to tell you to burn all of your possessions and trek into the rainforest in a loincloth to chew some roots while you rub an iguana on your forehead. This is simply a book about actions. If you're ready to develop practices in your life that help you handle difficult experiences as you take action to do things you care about, then this book is for you.

HOW THIS BOOK WORKS

This book is divided into two parts. The first part is all about learning basic mental health skills, and unlearning the ways of thinking and behaving that cause mental health challenges in our lives. The second part will help you make the switch from a fear-fuelled, anxiety-driven life to one that's based on your values, and is focused on creating and building what you want to see in your life instead of trying to avoid and control what you don't want to see.

At the end of all of the chapters except for the last one, you'll find an exercise. *Do the exercises* – don't simply read them. When you actually do the exercises in this book, not only will they become more useful to you, but you'll be able to engage more with the content of the book because you'll have shared the experience of tackling the challenges I discuss.

Some of the exercises are there to underpin changes you may need to make to your life. They're human-centred design and change-management exercises adapted from the business world. Improving and maintaining great mental health and fitness is a big, complex process but don't let that put you off. It's similar to complex changes companies are making all of the time to innovate successfully. We can apply the same tools to innovate in our own lives.

So test the exercises: play around with them, get them to work in your life. Focus on what works to help you with the challenges you're overcoming in your life. Find where your limitations are and use these exercises to push into what's difficult. Modify them. Talk about them.

Now, before you're tempted to head straight to Chapter 1, bear with me – the following section is important.

THE FUNDAMENTAL EMOTIONAL FITNESS EXERCISE

There are many different ways to improve your cardiovascular fitness. You can run, bike, swim, play table tennis, do interval training, lift weights, do jazzaerobics, whatever. Any exercise for cardiovascular health does one very specific thing: it raises your heart rate. Weightlifting is also about a variety of ways to do one simple thing: put tension on your muscles. You do that until it's difficult to continue. And then you do it some more.

There are fundamental principles to improving your physical fitness, regardless of the exercise. Physical fitness is about finding that moment of discomfort, feeling it, believing it means you can't go further and need to stop, but then pushing on through. Keep that in mind with emotional fitness.

I define emotional fitness as your capacity to experience emotions while continuing to make choices aligned with your values. It's analogous to cardiovascular fitness. It's an indicator of your ability to keep taking steps towards your goals in life while experiencing whatever emotions come up. It's not about avoiding feelings or controlling them. It's actually about feeling much *more*.

The fundamental practice, when working on our emotional fitness, is to stay with whatever internal or external experience is occurring and then follow it up by doing something you value. Essentially that means pushing into experiences you find difficult while you practise being yourself. To continue the exercise analogy, instead of increasing your heart rate while continuing with an exercise, you increase your feelings while still functioning.

As you adapt the skills and concepts from this book to fit into your own life, always keep that fundamental exercise in mind.

FAIL

As with physical fitness, failing is part of improving your emotional fitness. If you find the exercises in this book difficult, that's wonderful! If you fail at them, great! Keep going. Those moments that feel impossible are actually when change happens. In a sense, taking on any fitness challenge is impossible with the brain or the body we have, but pushing through them in a healthy way changes us, and we develop the body and brain we *need* to make overcoming those challenges possible.

Have you ever done a burpee? It's a deceptively cute-sounding exercise. To do one, you drop your chest to the ground, push up into a plank, jump your feet forward to your hands, then jump up in the air, clap your hands over your head, drop back down into a plank, and bring your chest to the floor again. At the gym I attend, the workout of the day sometimes includes fifty burpees as a warm-up.* We do them ten at a time, with a thirty-second break between each set.

Fifty burpees used to sound like a complete workout to me, not a warm-up. If I had tried to do fifty burpees, I would have failed. I would've ended up with my head between my knees, gasping for breath and trying not to vomit. But now, because I've failed

---

* Thanks to Blair and all of the coaches at CrossFit YKV for always pushing me to pick up the bar when I think I can't.

through many workouts that included burpees, I can do them. All of the failures helped me get to a point where fifty burpees are a warm-up. This is as relevant to mental health and emotional fitness as it is to physical fitness. Even when practising skills like meditation or mindfulness, which we'll get to in the first part of the book, if you're new to them, expect to fail often at them. The capacity to do anything is on the other side of failure.

Those anxiety-ridden experiences of failure can become ways to measure progress, not by decreasing them, but by increasing them. Instead of letting anxieties and uncertainties fence off your life, they can become signposts showing you where to turn to do what really matters to you.

If you avoid sweating, eventually everything makes you sweat. If you avoid anxiety, eventually everything makes you anxious.

SUPPORT YOUR EMOTIONAL FITNESS PRACTICE

When you embark on any process of complex change, it's important to gather supports in your life for that journey. Here are a few supports that can help you with implementing the changes we'll explore:

Peer support

Connect with people on similar journeys to your own. They might have done the journey at a different time, or taken a slightly different route, but they'll have insights into the challenges ahead of you and, most importantly, how to overcome them.

No matter how unique you may think your struggle is, many people have overcome the exact same issues, and many people are doing the work to overcome them right now, all around you. Connect with them. ▶

Food

You run on energy. Whether you're a human, a robot or a tomato plant, you need energy to do anything. If you're doing a strenuous activity, you need *more* energy. Making changes in your life is an incredibly strenuous activity. So fuel that practice. You can't have mental health without food.

It's important to note here that food can easily become wrapped up in the types of behaviour that make mental health worse. As we explore those behaviours throughout the book, consider how they apply to the way you eat. Watch out that you are not trying to use food as a magic pill to solve mental health challenges. If you think you've discovered a too-good-to-be-true diet that promises to make anxiety and depression disappear, it's far more likely that all you've discovered is a potential eating disorder to slap on top of your existing issues.

Eat to fuel being yourself and doing what you love.

Exercise

Exercise is another support, similar to food, that you can use in a way that benefits your mental health or makes it worse. It is not a replacement for the changes you need to make. You can be in amazing physical shape while also struggling with serious mental health challenges. When we start thinking that simply exercising more will fix the problems in our life, we're slipping back into the trap of searching for a magic pill that will solve all of our troubles.

Sleep

You have to have adequate sleep. Not only is it necessary for everyday functioning, but particularly when ▶

you're doing something like changing your brain – which is what we're going to be doing – you need to sleep. It allows your brain to flush out all of the toxins that build up in there during the day, and allows it to build new connections and absorb the things you're learning. Sleep helps you handle your emotions better: you can react less and be less disturbed by things that normally might bother you.[1] As we get to exercises on accepting feelings or thoughts that you might have avoided in the past, having enough sleep will help to make them a little bit easier.

Your breath

This is the most important support you'll need on this journey. Your breath is your unbreakable tether to the present. You'll often forget that it's there, but you can always find it again, right where you left it. Come back to your breath when you encounter a challenge, or when you meet something beautiful, or when you take a step. If you notice you're floating off into the past or the future, follow your breath back to the path.

A recovery-focused therapist

It's so important that any therapist you work with has a focus on recovery and helping you do the things you want to do in life. If you get a therapist who says you've got a chronic disease and all you will ever do is manage it, that's like asking a personal trainer to help you train for a marathon and him telling you it's not possible, you'll never be able to do it and that the most you can hope to do is manage the symptoms of being out of shape – have you tried diet pills?

Personally, I wouldn't recommend working with ▶

> that trainer. In the same way, I wouldn't recommend working with a similarly negative healthcare practitioner. If you work with a professional on your fitness goals, whatever they may be, make sure that professional has a demonstrable track record of helping their patients to achieve the goals you're pursuing.

BE EMPOWERED

Take responsibility for making changes and empower yourself to make them. Recognising that you can make changes to improve and maintain your mental health is not about blaming yourself for mental health challenges you're experiencing. It's about taking back the power that anxiety and fear rob us of.

I was very lucky when I finally found help that I worked with Dr Maureen Whittal and one of her students. They never suggested that I couldn't get over the challenges with which I was struggling. They expected recovery, and they gave me the tools to recover.

When I hear people say that mental illness is a chronic disease, it's as strange to me as if there were people standing outside a gym shouting: 'Exercise is a sham! You'll be out of shape for ever! You're unfit because you have a chemical imbalance!'

We know how to help people get into great physical shape. You can go to any gym and see people who have access to the skills and knowledge to do that. We're already at the same point with recovery from mental illness. People recover from OCD, they recover from schizophrenia,[2] they recover from Borderline Personality Disorder (BPD),[3] they recover from eating disorders,[4] they recover from depression,[5] they recover from addiction.[6] But just like physical fitness, it doesn't happen through magic. You have to work at it. Not everybody succeeds, which is why I'm sharing this book with you so you're more prepared to take on this challenge. Of course, not everyone has a mental 'illness' but the same applies: even if we are simply seeking the ability to handle anxiety in our lives – it requires effort.

Feeling empowered to make a change can still seem like a daunting task. But one of the most beneficial lessons I learned on my own journey was that I could make changes everywhere, even with seemingly normal, everyday activities. With the first exercise we'll dive into, below, you'll get to see how an activity you do many times daily (possibly over a hundred times each day) can be an opportunity to make changes that support your mental health. This exercise covers many of the fundamental techniques that we'll build upon in the chapters ahead.

EXERCISE: Learn how to catch an urge

The most basic mental fitness skill is learning how to catch an urge, accept it, and then make a conscious, mindful decision about what you want to do. Everything we practise after this is simply an extension of accepting your internal experience and making a healthy decision. If you can master this skill, your productivity, your ability to pay attention to the people you care about, your ability to make decisions that support your romantic relationships, and your ability to use your free time in a way that makes you feel good about yourself can all improve. You'll be able to handle whatever pops into your head, no matter how intense, keep your attention where you want to focus it, and make choices to build long-term health and happiness instead of reacting impulsively to short-term discomfort.

One of the simplest ways to practise this exercise is with your mobile phone (but you can adapt it to anything you do automatically, such as checking things on your computer, automatically turning on the TV when you get home, etc.). Here's how it works:

1. **Carry your phone with you at all times.** There's nothing wrong with having a phone on you. It's how you interact with it that causes the problems.
2. **Experience the urge to check your phone.** Maybe you want to see if you received a text message you were waiting for, or maybe you want to check for a response to an important email, or your lottery numbers, or your dating profile for a message from 'the one' – whatever it is, don't try to get rid of the urge, but also *don't check your phone!* Feel the uncertainty. So much of improving your mental health is about learning to handle uncertainty.
3. **Choose when you want to check your phone.** This is about putting you back in charge of how you spend your time and energy. Urges don't have to dictate your actions. You are not a dog. You do not have to chase every stick your brain throws for you. When you notice the urge to check your phone, accept that urge – it's totally fine for it to be there – but set a time and place when you'll check it. And then follow through on that, whether you feel you need to or not when that time arrives.
4. **Practise.** Keep practising until you no longer check your phone as an automatic reaction to the urge to check. Only use your phone when you choose to use it. You may need to practise this exercise for a week or two before it begins to be normal. But only go back to reacting to the urges your brain throws at you if compulsively reacting to urges is something at which you hope to become incredibly skilled.

If you don't feel you have a problem with checking your phone, or it's not something that bothers you, that's great. This should be very easy for you then. But try this exercise before you decide it's not a struggle for you. If you can learn how to handle a simple uncertainty like, 'Did I get an email?' you'll be much more prepared to handle a big uncertainty like, 'Should I end this relationship?' or 'What if I'm about to die?' If you find that not checking your phone causes you noticeable discomfort, or that you check it so automatically you don't even notice quickly enough to stop yourself, keep an open mind to the possibility that there are other behaviours in your life you're unaware of that are contributing to poor mental health and fitness.

> IF YOU AVOID SWEATING, EVENTUALLY EVERYTHING MAKES YOU SWEAT
>
> IF YOU AVOID ANXIETY, EVENTUALLY EVERYTHING MAKES YOU ANXIOUS

PART ONE

The Basics

STEP 1

Understand that you are not a rock

I want to share a true story with you. It's about some rocks, and it goes like this:

One day, early in the twenty-first century, up on a mountain in the Italian Alps, there were two very large rocks. They sat on the side of a mountain, overlooking a farm on the road between Ronchi and Cortaccia, Strada Provinciale 19 (in case you're planning a roadtrip).

On that particular day, there were external, contextual factors affecting the rocks, factors over which they had no control. Those contextual factors caused a landslide. And the rocks fell off the mountain.

They tumbled down the slope towards the farm. There was a single-lane country road at the bottom of the slope, running alongside the farmhouse and the adjoining barn. One of the rocks landed on the road and stopped, directly in front of the entrance to the farmhouse. It was a massive rock. It reached up to the roof of the farmhouse. With some extra momentum, it would have destroyed the house and everything (and everybody) inside.

The other, similarly enormous rock, however, didn't stop at the road. It rolled right across it, into the old barn on the other side. The force of the impact destroyed the barn, scattering wall planks and whole sections of the roof across the yard. The rock continued on down into the valley, getting an inefficient head-start on the annual wine pressing, finally coming to rest beside an even larger rock that had fallen off the mountain many years before.

If rocks could feel, how do you think that rock would have felt after it did that? Embarrassed? Guilty? Desperate to blame the landslide? Angry at the other rock for not following through on their plan? Do you think that other rock obsessed about the carnage it would have caused if it hadn't stopped when it did?

How would you have felt if you were either of those rocks? Have you ever spent an hour thinking about what to write in a text message because you were afraid of saying the wrong thing and ruining a relationship? Have you reread and rewritten work emails, over and over again, anxious about getting fired or seeming incompetent? Does responsibility make you anxious? Do you spend days obsessing about mistakes in your past? Do you wish you could get rid of those memories? Do you hear people in your head shouting at you for screwing up? Do you spend hours trying to rationalise why you're not to blame for things going wrong in your life?

So here's my point: those are all very human experiences. Those rocks in that valley in Italy will never have any of those experiences. I said '*If* rocks could feel'. They can't, they're rocks. You are not a rock. You feel things.

BE HUMAN

You probably approach physical fitness like a human. If you want to build strength, you lift heavy things that make you feel weak. If you want to increase endurance, you run until you're sweating and aching and ready to stop, and you keep running a little bit further so that next time it won't be so difficult. If you want to be more flexible, you stretch into stiffness again and again until your flexibility increases. You try to go beyond last week's limits. You fail and fail and call it 'practice'. You do squats and deadlifts until your legs are wobbly and so sore the next day that you can't stand up, and you call that a 'good workout'.

This paradoxical practice of doing a difficult thing so that the difficult thing becomes less difficult is how humans change. This is a concept most people understand. If you told somebody that you plan to become stronger by avoiding strenuous exercise, even people who don't exercise would know that was ridiculous.

But there are probably many people around you that encourage you to approach mental health in the exact opposite way. They tell you not to do the difficult things. Avoid anxiety, feel less stress, don't think bad thoughts, watch out for triggers, get rid of uncertainty, man up, don't be so emotional, don't feel bad (everything will be OK). This is not how humans develop their ability to handle difficult challenges. Trying to avoid difficult things makes difficult things more difficult.

This is so important to understand as you start to build better emotional fitness. You can develop your ability to handle emotions by feeling more, and especially by feeling more of the feelings that challenge you. By lifting heavy emotions, lifting heavy emotions becomes easier. You can feel a greater range of emotions and you can feel them more deeply.

Poor mental health doesn't fall from the sky. Mental illness is like heart disease – you work your way up to it through a complex mix of environmental, genetic and educational factors combined with each decision you make at home, at work, at school, in relationships – wherever you might be, every single minute of the day. Turning away from feelings, trying to control them, cover them up or chase after them are the deep-fried pepperoni sticks, triple-decker cheeseburgers and super-sized pizzas of the mental health world. Sure, you might crave them, and they'll feel good, and you'll never be able to blame a specific junk food for giving you a heart attack, but when they become a regular part of your everyday life the end results are always nasty.

In these first two chapters, I'll cover two concepts that are fundamental to building better mental health and emotional fitness. It's important that we have a shared idea about what exercises for mental health look like and why we do them. So I'll repeat:

You are not a rock. You feel things.

I WANTED TO BE A ROCK

In the past, I constantly chose to do things, inside my head and outside it, to not feel things. I didn't want to feel uncertain, or hated, or alone, or broke, or trapped, or ugly, or hurt, or unhappy, or guilty, or anxious... There were so many feelings I didn't want to feel! I basically wanted to be a rock.

Rocks don't have varying levels of improvable mental health. Rocks don't imagine stabbing other rocks. Rocks don't get jealous, or struggle with their sexuality, or question the meaning of existence. Rocks don't convince themselves that other rocks are trying to poison them.

When we're trying not to feel things, we're trying to be rocks. So it's not surprising that we sink the moment we're thrown into uncertainty. Rocks sink.

Rocks will always feel less anxiety than you. They will beat you every single time at feeling less guilt and regret. No rock will ever make as many mistakes as you will. No matter how much you practise meditation, you will always be more easily distracted and less focused than the most mediocre pebble in a muddy ditch. You will never worry as little as a rock worries. You will never be able to suppress your cravings as well as a rock does. No rock will ever relapse as many times as you do. No rock will ever fail as many times as you fail.

As you work through the exercises in this book and you live your life, remember that rock* in that vineyard in Italy not thinking or feeling about the antique barn it obliterated. You are not like that rock. You cannot be like that rock. You can spend your entire life trying to be like that rock but you'll only make yourself more miserable, and you'll probably destroy much more than a barn.

You cannot build better mental health by trying to avoid being human. If you want to improve your mental health, it won't happen through wanting to avoid uncertainty, anxiety and all the other feelings you don't like. It'll happen by learning how to have those experiences. If you want to avoid human experiences, this is not the book for you. If you continue to pursue escape from those experiences, you will only have more of them, at ever increasing levels of severity and complexity.

WHAT IS YOUR GOAL?

We often set goals for ourselves that might be better suited for rocks than humans. We want to feel less anxiety, we want to feel less guilt, less sadness, to obsess less, to engage in compulsions less, be less lonely, less paranoid ... But we will never be able to do any of those as well as rocks do. Have you ever seen a rock addicted to drugs or gambling? I haven't either. Rocks are so disciplined!

Understanding that I am not a rock frames how I approach every mental health issue in my life. As a human, I can feel and think things I don't like. Translating this understanding into actions has been an incredible support for overcoming mental illness and continuing to improve my mental health. In particular, it shapes the goals I pursue. For you, with your mental health, and even with this book, I strongly recommend that you *don't pursue goals that rocks can do better than you.*

* 46°19'22.5"N 11°14'02.0"E

Avoiding unhappiness is not the same as experiencing happiness. You can pour the rest of your life into trying not to be anxious and trying to prevent your worries from coming true, and all you'll have done is focus your energy on things that didn't happen and you didn't even want to think about. Use this book to do things that rocks can't do better than you. And to help you do that, use the next exercise to set some creative *human* goals. These will be goals to keep in mind throughout the rest of the book and beyond. Each of the subsequent chapters will help equip you with the knowledge and the skills to achieve these goals. But as you take steps towards your goals, always reflect on this question: Am I trying to do something that a rock can do better than me?

EXERCISE: Creative Human Goals

Rocks can do anything less than you can. But they can't do anything more than you can. So rather than setting goals around what you want to avoid, it can help to set goals around the things you want to build and create. Health is creative, not destructive. That doesn't mean we don't eliminate barriers, such as compulsive behaviours that get in the way of us achieving our goals, but eliminating barriers isn't the end-state. Unhealthy behaviours simply become things we don't do anymore because we're spending our time and energy on creating health and happiness and a life that's aligned with our values.

So grab something to write with, and articulate creative human goals for yourself that rocks can't do better than you. Here are a couple of ideas to help you:

- If you had one overarching goal for your entire life, what would it be? If you looked at the different areas in your life, such as health, relationships, work, education, etc., what would your goal be for each? What

Understand that you are not a rock 25

would your goal be for today? What's your goal for this moment right now? Take a look at the examples below, comparing goals for rocks and goals for humans, to see some possible directions for your goals:

Goals for rocks	Goals for humans
I'll use this book to learn how to get rid of anxiety so I can finally start doing things I care about.	I'll use this book to learn how to handle more anxiety while I do things I care about.
Not be lonely anymore.	Attend at least one group social event every week.
I don't want people to judge me.	Be more accepting of others out on the street and online.
Stop feeling so much guilt and regret.	Learn how to practise feeling compassion towards myself and others.
Get rid of this uncertainty about whether my partner loves me or not.	Practise expressing myself honestly in a relationship, even when I'm afraid of being hurt.

- In any situation it's possible to have a goal you're working towards, even if that goal is simply to breathe. The goals we carry into a situation shape our expectations. Aligning our experience with our expectations determines whether we laugh, shout or cry. So, what is your goal with this book? Did you pick up this book in the hope of getting rid of a feeling? Because every rock is already much better than you when it comes to not experiencing that feeling. What's something that only you can do? What's something that you care about that you want to do more of in your life? How will you know if you've achieved that goal?

Make sure your goals are visible. Put them where you'll see them. You might want to write them out on individual pieces of paper so you can put relevant goals where they're more likely to remind you to take action. If you have a goal to sleep more, maybe you need to stick that to your computer so you remember to go to sleep earlier. Take your work goals with you to work. If you have a goal to improve your capacity to experience anxiety, where can you put that goal, physically or digitally, as a reminder to push into anxiety instead of avoiding it?

STEP 2

Recognise your problems

> 'Most of my anxieties were linked with uncertainty and feeling uncomfortable. The amount of time and effort it took to avoid these feelings inevitably led to missing out on a ton of opportunities to do other things, things I loved and cared about. By exposing myself to uncomfortable experiences, I've learned that it is possible to accept uncertainty as part of life and stop wasting my time trying to avoid it or control it.'
>
> Daniela

The fact that it's a totally human experience to have feelings has implications for how we approach mental health. It means we're not going to invest our time and energy in trying to avoid or control thoughts or feelings. We can experience whatever happens in our heads. So the focus of our work to build better mental health and maintain it isn't targeted at symptom relief. Instead, we need to shift the focus to the problems that interfere with your ability to do what you want to do in life. We need to recognise our problems and not get caught up in the superficial symptoms. That's the second important concept we'll explore.

Again, this is something we understand with physical fitness.

Let's say I feel pain in my knee when I'm running, which persists even when I stop. I feel the pain the moment I wake up in the morning. That pain begins to interfere with everyday activities and eventually I can no longer do many of the activities I loved doing and associated with my identity. I'd probably go to a doctor or talk with a more experienced runner. They might give me some tips or, in the case of the doctor, prescribe something to relieve the pain, but I bet they would focus on why I'm experiencing that pain. It could be my gait, or how my foot hits the pavement, or the shoes I'm wearing, or maybe it's because of that time I fractured my ankle in a karate tournament as a teenager but didn't go to the doctor or tell anybody that my foot turned purple. Something I'm doing, or something that's happening, or something that happened to me in the past has led to the experience of that pain. Whatever it is, I need to look beyond the immediate pain and make changes around the problem(s) leading to that pain if I want to get back to exercising and functioning the way I want to function. I might have to unlearn how I've been running for years. I might have to work with a therapist doing intense, often painful exercises to rehabilitate the knee and learn healthier ways of running.

With physical fitness, that's how we would approach an issue that's interfering with my ability to function in life. We have to do the same with mental health issues.

Pain is a symptom. It might be something I feel, and something I don't want to feel, but focusing all of my energy on escaping it won't get rid of the root cause of that pain. In fact, if I try to eliminate the pain and I succeed, but I continue with everything I was doing before the pain started, it's entirely possible that the cause of the pain will worsen and do lasting damage in my life. This is especially true with mental health challenges.

Not only does relieving the symptoms of mental health issues have the potential to let those issues worsen, but they can worsen to a degree that effectively (or even literally) ends your life. Mental health issues are never benign. They're like a monster chewing on your leg. That's the kind of knee pain we're dealing with here. You could go to the doctor and try to get relief from that pain, but when there's a monster chewing your leg into hamburger meat, don't mistake relief from the pain of the monster's bite for escape from the monster's attack.

Too often, we go searching for relief from feelings we don't like and we find it. Then the monster moves on to chewing another part of us. Again, we seek out relief. The monster eats another part of us, the pain rises to our attention again and we find another way to relieve that pain. Eventually, the monster devours us completely.

Anxiety, depression, intrusive thoughts, craving, distress and all of the other feelings we dislike are types of pain. You can get rid of that pain if you want – there are many ways to do that and you've probably tried most of them. I tried most of them, too. And there are many situations when relief from pain is a key support for doing intense rehabilitation work, or empowering us to fight off the monsters chewing up our lives. But we also have to go after the source of the pain and make changes there.

If we're experiencing pain from mental health challenges, it can be very difficult to see past that pain and recognise the monster chewing on us. But we have to ask how our leg got into a monster's mouth in the first place, how we can get it out of there, and how we can prevent it from happening again in the future.

I can't tell you exactly what your monsters are. Be curious, and look past the pain to see the problems underneath. Sometimes those problems will be outside your direct control, in contextual factors like inequality or violence – monsters that leap out of the dark and attack you. Quite often, however, the problems will be things that you're doing. For instance, when you engage in compulsions, it's like walking up to a hungry monster and sticking your leg in its mouth. Of course the monster bites you. It's only natural you experience that pain.

WHAT IS A COMPULSION?

I'll be talking about compulsions throughout this book. They are the actions we engage in that make our mental health worse. I define a compulsion as *anything you do to cope with, check on or control uncertainty, anxiety and other feelings you don't like.* Understanding this has been the single biggest help with taking care of my mental health. If I engage in coping, checking and controlling behaviours, I'm choosing to experience more uncertainty, more anxiety and more of the feelings I don't like at ever-increasing levels of complexity and severity.

With compulsions, look for that pattern of coping, checking and controlling in reaction to unwanted experiences. Compulsions vary in their superficial characteristics. Some are the more stereotypical, overtly obvious compulsions we might associate with mental health issues, such as returning home to check that you have unplugged all of the appliances because you're afraid of causing a fire, or getting high every day to try to quieten the thoughts in your head, or shouting at people in the street because you think they're trying to steal your ideas, or sending your partner a deluge of text messages to be certain that they love you, or pulling out hair to cope with feelings you don't know how to handle or restricting what you eat as an attempt to control what you think others think about you. But compulsions can be present in any activity, like when we're checking our phones.

That first exercise we did, where you practised not checking your phone when you got the urge to check it, was about learning the basics of cutting out a compulsion. When you experience uncertainty about a message and you immediately check your phone to make that uncertainty go away, that's a compulsion, in a very simple, everyday, normal form.

Somebody might engage in compulsions by always controlling conversations and manipulating the truth as a way to control their fears about being disliked or not valued. That's not something obvious, like engaging in violence to control other people, but the rationale behind it is the same: there's a fear about something that could happen and then there's an attempt to control that fear.

Many compulsions 'work' phenomenally well, although for shorter and shorter periods of time until eventually they don't work at all. They get rid of the immediate pain, but they always cause more pain in the long term. You don't solve anything with compulsions. Your 'solutions' are part of the problem. They lead to more pain. You can see this pattern at work any time you procrastinate.

I WAS AN OLYMPIC-LEVEL PROCRASTINATOR

I was an impressively skilled procrastinator for much of my life. At university I took a Chinese poetry course to fill a degree requirement. This was at a point in my university career when I was playing lots of video games, spending hours online and was involved in so many extracurricular activities that I usually neglected those as well. With all of those important things to do, there was no time left for studying. I only did school work when the panicked pressure of failing became so intolerable that I would actually pick up a book.

I fell behind in my classes. That made me anxious. With that increase in anxiety, I spent even more time trying to escape the pressure.

Thinking about the amount of reading for poetry class felt like I was trying to tickle a panic attack out of my stomach. I held on to the belief that I was so smart I could always pull an all-nighter and study whatever I needed to know for the final exam. I could handle a thousand years of Chinese poetry in a night. Sheer terror and arrogance are a potent mixture of emotions that accomplish amazing disasters.

In the final weeks of the term, I went to the last class of Chinese poetry to find out what was in the exam so I could masterfully cram it into my brain. I loved that professors always covered the exam topics in the last class.

I walked into the windowless cinderblock box of a classroom and I remember noticing that the room seemed abnormally full, even though there were still several minutes before class started. I sat down to wait and the professor came in a little while later; he immediately began handing out exam papers.

This kind professor had offered to do an in-class exam before the normal exam period so that everybody could focus on their exams for other (arguably more important) classes. What a nice professor! Such a diligent class of poetry students! And oh my God, there was literally no way I could bluff my way through the exam because I hadn't read any of the poems. I didn't know my Li Yu from my Hanshan. I didn't even know those were things I didn't know.

If I'd read any of the poems for the class, I'm sure I could have recited one at that moment to express precisely how I felt. But since I hadn't, all I was left with was the panicked poetry of my heart thumping at rib cage-busting intensity. The feeling of anxiety in my body had gone from its usual 100 to 100 trillion in a second. My face probably flushed an amazing shade red. I don't remember what I said to the professor – I think I told him I felt sick, which wasn't exactly a lie at that moment. He agreed to let me leave and do the exam later. Somehow, I passed the course. To that very wonderful professor: 谢谢!

I was very stressed afterwards, which was completely natural given the months of compulsions I'd invested in avoiding all of the feelings I didn't like: the difficulty, the boredom and, later, the anxiety.

Pain is a totally natural outcome of those avoidance compulsions. It's very normal to feel pain when a monster bites you. It's very normal to feel even more anxiety when you try to avoid things that make you anxious. If you want to run a marathon but you don't feel like training, and you don't start practising until a few weeks before the race when you feel the pressure of that approaching deadline, what will your experience be like when you're running that marathon? Probably painful. The problem, however, is not the marathon or the pain or the exhaustion you feel. The problem was the months of avoiding practice before the marathon. The problem probably felt good. It wasn't distressing. You probably had reasons to put off that practice. It seemed rational.

Had I gone to get help in the week following that stressful exam experience, I might have presented the pain and stress as the problem. I had a panic attack in class! I was stressed about exams! Anxious about my grades! What could I do to get rid of that anxiety? But asking that is like somebody mid-marathon asking how to be less exhausted or to feel less pain. I would've been seeking help for a symptom that's only a natural result of months invested in a problem.

BREAK THE COMPULSION ADDICTION

Here's the thing with compulsions: even though we engage in them as an attempt to cope with, check and control experiences we don't like, compulsions become their own problem. And as with any addiction, when you start to cut them out, you experience all of the pain from all of the monster bites that you were using them to avoid.

Along with setting out the basic principles of mental health and emotional fitness, the first several chapters of this book focus on helping you to better understand how coping, checking and controlling as reactions to uncertainty and other feelings you don't like are actually fuelling those experiences. They always cause more of what you're trying to avoid.

In the past, I experienced lots of pain around other people. A lot of that pain had to do with wanting other people not to dislike me. That's something that's very difficult to be certain about, because I don't know what other people are thinking and nor can I control what they're thinking. So I would do many things that I believed would help prevent me from being disliked. For instance, I tried to avoid expressing opinions or likes or dislikes. I quickly discounted whatever I cared about. I liked whatever you liked. I disliked whatever you disliked. We like the same things! We hate the same things! Let's be friends!

My reaction to the pain was to do things that only allowed the problem to worsen. That's a very common reaction. Instead of recognising the compulsions – such as lying to others to try to get them to like me – I spent years focused on the symptoms created by the compulsions: stress, fatigue, fear, anxiety, depression, conflict, loneliness. Being so caught up in the compulsions prevented me from ever dealing with the underlying issues I had around other people. I was so hooked on trying to get people to like me, I never addressed my fears about being alone or disliked. So those fears deepened.

Nothing changed until I started eliminating the compulsions. Then I had to address the problems I'd been hiding beneath them.

To help you clear out the compulsions so you can begin to get at what's underneath, this chapter's exercise will explore how you're doing what you're doing in your life. You'll also look at what you want to be doing in your life. Clearly articulating those two things will give you your starting point and destination for the journey of building better mental health.

EXERCISE: The Inventories

We're going to do two connected exercises: The Inventory and The Ideal Inventory. They're visual data-collection exercises about your life. The Inventory is very simple but powerful. It works like this:

1. Grab a pen and some paper, or a notebook or sticky-notes – whatever you like. Make sure it's tangible and relatively permanent. It needs to be something you can pull out later and look at. This is not an

exercise you can do in your head. You can do this digitally if you want, but read through the entire exercise first and make sure your digital tools won't restrict you.
2. Write down or draw how you spend your time and energy in life. This is not what you want to be true, but what *is* true about you, right now, at this point in your life. Show it all.

You might have the urge to censor yourself, but just ignore that little voice in your head. Don't worry about anyone else seeing this – you have complete permission to hide this away in your deepest, darkest sock drawer, or to burn it when you've finished using it. So get the words out of your head. Here's how I do it:

If you're struggling with alcohol, show how much time and energy gets spent on that struggle. Do you cook all the time? Write that down. What do you often cook? Speak Portuguese at home and English at work? Get it on there. Spend a couple of hours every day fantasising about a colleague and surreptitiously visiting their social media profiles? Show how much of your waking hours that takes up. What do you do in the mornings? What do you do in your head all day? How do you interact with other people? How much of your life do you control? Try to capture everything about how you spend your time and energy.

Show relationships between activities. Do some activities happen inside other activities? When I do this exercise I like to draw blobs – I use their size, proximity and positioning to express meaning about the different activities.

Getting that all out in the open can make you feel nervous. I know I was shaking the first time I did this. I thought I'd spend about 30 minutes in a coffee shop writing it, and ended up staying there for two intense hours.

That first Inventory is only the beginning. After you've completed it, it's time for the Ideal Inventory. You'll create that with the same process but, this time, create your Inventory for the future. Imagine a day one year from now and visualise how you want to spend your time and energy on that day. What compulsions have you eliminated from your life so they don't even show up on your Ideal Inventory? What healthy activities have you introduced? What activities or people are only a tiny piece of your current Inventory but grow to a more significant portion of your Ideal Inventory?

When I first did my Ideal Inventory, I emphasised many of the activities I often thought about but didn't actually

Recognise your problems 37

do, or even know how to incorporate into my life, such as cooking, weight-lifting and meditation. I cut out all of the time I spent on compulsions. I added in much more time devoted to building social relationships. From doing the Inventory, it was also clear to me that I had the time to spend on doing things I loved, even if it was outside my work and schedule. My Ideal Inventory was realistic but firmly rooted in my passions.

[Hand-drawn mind map showing interconnected bubbles: CREATE (write, draw, code, make, build), SHARE ONLINE, WORK, VOLUNTEER WORK, COMMUNITY BUILDING, GIVE!, LAUNCH MY OWN BUSINESS, PROTECT THIS, READ ACTUAL BOOKS, LEARN, HONEST COMMUNICATION, HEALTHY RELATIONSHIPS (friends, family, romance), MEET PEOPLE, SLEEP, NUTRITION, BREAKFAST!, MEAL PREP + GROCERIES, EXERCISE (weight lifting, yoga, 5k training), MEDITATION, PRACTISE NON-JUDGEMENT, ACCEPT THE STUFF IN MY HEAD]

When you've completed both Inventories, take some time to reflect on the gap between the two of them. That gap is your journey ahead. All of the skills and concepts we cover in this book will help you take the journey between those two points.

Don't mistake relief from the pain of the monster's bite, for escape from the monster's attack

STEP 3

Practise mindfulness

'To understand how to accept the stuff in my head, it helped me to see it all as waves in the ocean. I don't choose when a thought can just stop, similarly to how I can't choose when a wave crashes . . . But it always does crash, just in its own time. Sometimes the waves grow higher. Sometimes the waves are smaller. Sometimes waves take longer to crash, and sometimes they crash right away. What waves pop up and when they crash is not something under my control. If I were to jump into the ocean and try to stop every wave, I would achieve nothing. All that is achieved is wasted energy and frustration. Same goes with trying to control the stuff in my head.'

Suzanne

We've covered two important concepts so far:

1. We feel things because we're human.
2. We need to focus on solving problems, not symptoms.

Now we get to a fundamental practice: *mindfulness*. You'll find this practice in every exercise we do to build emotional fitness, because we need to be present with our emotions if we want to learn how to handle them better and handle more of the emotions we don't like so we can do the things in life that matter to us. Taking care of our mental health is all about learning to accept the stuff in our heads without judgement as we make decisions in the present that help us to be happy and healthy over the long term. Mindfulness is a practice that will help you accept the stuff in your head without judgement. The amazing thing is, when you accept your internal experiences – when you're not judging a thought as bad, or a feeling as wrong, or an uncertainty as something that needs resolving – you'll eliminate much of what characterises any struggle with mental health. If you're challenged by the stuff in your head, mindfulness will be a very useful practice to bring into your life. But like anything, it's only useful if you practise it.

Dr Jon Kabat-Zinn, the professor, meditation teacher and researcher who developed Mindfulness-based Stress Reduction (MBSR), a therapeutic approach to applying mindfulness in clinical settings, gives a 'working' definition of mindfulness that I find very useful: *'mindfulness is the awareness that arises through paying attention on purpose in the present moment – non-judgmentally'*.[7] I like that definition because it explains mindfulness in a way that makes it accessible at any time. You can pay attention on purpose wherever you are. It's also an action we do non-judgementally. As we'll explore later, judgement is the spark that sets off the chain reaction of anxiety, fear and compulsions with which we so often find ourselves struggling.

That definition also emphasises the importance of intention. Taking care of your health does not happen by accident. You're responsible and empowered to practise mindfulness. If you don't choose to practise mindfulness, it's not strange if your mind is constantly wandering off. It's not weird if you struggle to pay attention. It's not surprising if your mind is always throwing thoughts at you about things you don't want to think about. Those are all natural consequences of practising mindlessness.

MINDLESSNESS IS A PRACTICE, TOO

To understand mindfulness better, it can help to explore its opposite: mindlessness. If we flip Kabat-Zinn's definition of mindfulness, we could say that mindlessness means not paying attention in any particular way; unintentionally, lost in the past or the future, judging everything.

A morning full of practising mindlessness might go something like this. You wake up and immediately begin checking messages on your phone while you lie in bed, flipping through news stories looking for something interesting until you feel the pressure of being late push you to get up. Then you tweet on the toilet before going to watch the news and write emails while you talk to your partner over breakfast as you have conversations in your head with co-workers you need to meet later that day about a project that's alarmingly behind schedule.

The imaginary conversations with your co-workers continue on your commute to work, but turn into an argument because you know Susan from HR can't take any criticism and she'll blame you for everything going wrong, even though it wasn't your fault and you told people at the start of the project that this would happen. Why does nobody listen to you?!

You're oblivious to the drive to your office, only snapping out of the argument in your head to honk at a guy in a sports car who cuts you up. The accident that nearly happened flashes through your head. You know exactly what type of idiot drives a car like that.

When you rush into the office, late for your morning departmental meeting, your body still feels as if it's out on the street, about to get in a fight with that other driver. You can feel the tightness in your chest and the butterflies you always get when you confront people. That is mixed in with the buzz of anxiety in the back of your head, reminding you that you've got a report to finish that you promised to send to a client later today.

All of those feelings are only exacerbated by the complete and utter hopelessness that this meeting you're now in could produce anything remotely useful. Your body might be in that meeting, smiling at what people are saying, but in your mind you're compiling a list of all the tasks you need to do to get that report finished.

As soon as the meeting is over, you rush to the kitchen to grab a coffee so you can try to wake up a bit, before collapsing at your desk. You feel stressed from the morning. The work you've got ahead of you for the day seems daunting. There's so much data to collect and analyse and you find that so tedious.

You flip through your social media accounts for a few minutes. You know you'll feel the urge to check them later so you want to get that out of the way. After half an hour you put on a podcast for some background noise, open up the report document and get started.

At least, you want to get started, but it's difficult to focus. You write a few sentences, and then you pull out your phone again without even noticing you've done so, checking your social media accounts again, then your email. There aren't any new messages. You check them all again. Then there is a new message! You respond to it, then get back to the report. It's agonisingly difficult to focus on it. You go online to look for jobs that pay well but won't require many extra qualifications. Maybe you should become a software developer? You read an article online recently about how much developers get paid. Software start-up offices have ping-pong tables and you would love to play ping-pong at work ...

PRACTISE GIVES YOU SKILLS

That was mindlessness at work: your mind constantly jumping to a different place and time, judging everything, reacting to those judgements, relying on anxiety about the past and the future to fuel all of your actions, bouncing from one crisis to the next. If you look at everything in that example leading up to the moment you wanted to start work on that report, it's not at all surprising that focusing on work was difficult. The practice of mindlessness, like any practice, has totally natural consequences: your brain gets better at it and wants to do it even more. Brains like to do the things they do repeatedly. It's easy. It saves energy. After hours of priming your mind to not be present, it's normal for it to continue functioning that way. How many hours over how many days have you committed to the practice of mindlessness?

If we spend all morning practising distraction, it's not a sign of illness if we then discover we can't do the things we want to do when we want to do them. If you have trouble paying attention and your days are in any way similar to what I've described above, you don't have an attention deficit disorder. Nor can you blame the internet or smartphones for being distracting. You have a brain. And your brain is a very good learner. It's doing exactly what you have trained it to do.

I spent years practising mindlessness. I was very skilled at it. Being mindless became my default mode in every situation, every day. I came to rely on that practice as the only way I knew how to function. I thought that way of living and working was helping me, but it was a maladaptive skill. I lost control of the monster I'd raised in my brain.

ALLOCATING BANDWIDTH FOR YOUR SEVEN SENSES

When we talk about extra senses, we're usually talking about paranormal powers, but this isn't about seeing ghosts or predicting the future. I assure you that this is totally grounded in a reality you're experiencing. Learning how to meditate and practise mindfulness in my daily life has helped me to recognise that I have seven senses. I experience sight, sound, touch, smell, taste, thought and emotion.

You sense your thoughts and emotions. They are not you. You experience them in the same way you experience a shout in the street, the sting of a wasp, a summer sunset, the reek of decay or the most delicious dessert melting on your tongue.

When we approach thoughts and emotions as senses, as experiences we can be aware of, it opens up the opportunity to move awareness around them. This is an especially useful skill to cultivate if you obsessively focus on thoughts spinning in your head or if you're overwhelmed by emotions.

You can probably remember an occasion when you were reading intently and didn't hear somebody call your name, or you were so engrossed in a movie that you forgot about the pain that kept you home from school that day. Or maybe you've noticed that staying constantly busy around other people seems to shut out all of the intrusive thoughts that bother you when you're alone. That's selective attention. We can't process all of the information coming to us from our senses at any given moment. Our awareness has a fixed amount of bandwidth for our senses. If we allocate all of the bandwidth to one or two senses, there's no space for the others.

You can experiment with this right now. Notice what your butt is in contact with. Be aware of that physical contact with whatever you're sitting or lying on right now. Or if you're standing crammed on public transport right now, notice the part of your body touching the person next to you. Awareness of that physical contact probably wasn't there a moment ago. You were reading or listening. Your awareness was concentrated on sight and thought. But the physical contact was still there. You simply weren't allocating any of your awareness bandwidth to that experience.

This ability to allocate bandwidth to your various senses is an ability you can develop and practise. It's an ability you've been constantly practising, every day, even if you weren't aware of it.

When we're struggling with the stuff in our head, we give all of that awareness bandwidth to those thoughts and emotions we want to avoid or control. That's a practice. We get skilled at it. There's only a tiny bit of bandwidth left over for processing the world around us and we become increasingly less skilled at that. So it becomes easier to ruminate about what we think our partner might have said than hearing what they actually did say. A memory from the past about an event that *didn't* happen can create more anxiety than something that *is* happening. The stuff in our heads becomes more real and meaningful than reality. Eventually it becomes a filter through which we experience our other senses, to such an extent that we only experience the filter. We get stuck bludgeoning every experience with the same distorted judgements, smothering everything with anxiety or mania or depression. The practice of mindfulness will give you the skills to choose how you allocate awareness to your experiences.

DOING WHAT YOU'RE DOING, BEING WHERE YOU'RE BEING

Mindfulness isn't a separate activity from our everyday lives. It's a way of doing and being. You don't need extra time in your life to practise mindfulness. In fact, you'll find it gives you more time because you'll actually be present for the life you're living. With mindlessness, you get stuck living a life that either won't happen or you wish didn't happen. When you're caught up in the practice of mindlessness, death becomes very frightening because you're acutely aware of moving closer and closer to the end of the life you could have had. Mindfulness is an opportunity to live.

To practise mindfulness, you simply keep your mind and body in the same place, doing what you're doing, being where you're being. If you're eating, eat. If you're listening, listen. If you're giving, give. If you're walking, walk. If you're driving, drive. If you're fucking, fuck. If you're singing, sing. If you're cooking, cook. If you're washing, wash.

We can find incredible enjoyment in the present moment when we're present to experience that enjoyment, doing whatever we're doing.

BUT WON'T MINDFULNESS SLOW ME DOWN? I HAVE THINGS TO DO!

The practice of mindfulness might sound like it won't fit into your hectic life. It might seem as if you're being asked to give up the time you spend solving problems in your head, preparing for conversations and coming up with all of your best ideas. How can anybody accomplish anything if they're not on their phone texting their partner while eating their lunch and writing an email to their boss at the same time as they're working on next year's budget spreadsheet and responding to notifications from their social media accounts? Life is designed for twelve hands and three heads, but we only have one brain so that brain needs to do more. If you can't send important emails sitting on your toilet at 2 a.m., you'll get left behind . . .

The reality is that practising mindfulness will help you get more done. When I struggled with my mental health, my brain was constantly spinning this hamster wheel of aggressively anxious thoughts, which only made me even more anxious and miserable. I was stressed all of the time by my own doing. I had to give up so much energy just to deal with how upset I was constantly making myself. Now that I don't do that anymore, I have so much more energy to put into doing what I actually care about.

Confirmation bias makes it easy for us to remember the great idea we came up with while totally distracted from doing something else. We can easily forget all of the times we've made ourselves miserable and anxious and upset ruminating about something in the past or what might happen in the future while our bodies were left to run on autopilot in the present.

> EXERCISE: **Everyday Mindfulness**
>
> Mindfulness is something you can practise every day. You have the opportunity, in any moment, to be present. You can feel what you're feeling and experience what you're

experiencing as you do what you're doing. Practise within the context in which you live. I'll share some different situations here in which you can try practising mindfulness to explore it

Mindful Mobility

Whether you walk, use a wheelchair, run, bike, drive, fly or move by any other means, try practising mindfulness while you do it.

Of all the activities I now do to maintain my mental health, mindful walking has been the most enjoyable discovery. I didn't know it was possible to walk without constantly spinning the hamster wheel of thoughts in my head. Why did nobody tell me I didn't have to spend every walk anxiously ruminating?

In the past, I intentionally approached walking as a time to obsess, to stay inside my head and shut out my other senses. I wouldn't see or hear anything around me because I was too busy debating in my head with politicians I disagreed with, or trying to explain to an ex why it was their fault we broke up, or digging in my memories for evidence that would prove I hadn't committed a crime or done something mean to a friend. When I wasn't focused inwards, I'd let my brain run all over the world around me, like a deranged, untrained puppy, sniffing and judging and pissing on everything.

Moving through the world mindfully is about being present to your experience now. It's about keeping that rambunctious puppy brain beside you, not running off to the past or the future. It's about being aware of the world and the experience you're having in it.

Notice how judgements pop into your head. Can you recognise those judgements but not chase after them? Try moving your awareness around your senses. Instead of allocating attention to thoughts or judgements, can you practise giving more bandwidth to awareness of sounds? Or what you see? Or the movement of your body in the present moment?

There is incredible enjoyment to discover in moving through the world mindfully, whether you're going out on a hot date, or to the most important business meeting of your life, or to the shop to buy loo roll.

Mindful Listening

Today, or sometime in the week ahead, try entering into a conversation with the intention of practising mindful listening. Be there with the person or people with whom you're having the conversation. When you notice yourself chasing after thoughts, starting to worry about how you look, or whether you're being understood, or what you should say next so the other person thinks you're smart or funny, or if there's something in your teeth, or that the person you're speaking to is mocking you, or whether there's somebody more interesting you could be talking to, simply bring your awareness back to the present. Listen. Listen to what they say without attaching judgements and extra baggage from your past to their words. Give understanding instead of trying to get it. Can you bring enjoyment to simply listening, instead of approaching each conversation like a danger to avoid or a problem to solve?

As you begin this practice, it might only be about noticing how much stuff you're doing in your head. It might be very difficult to stop doing all of that stuff and simply listen. That's OK. Be mindful of the difficulty. You don't have to judge yourself for it. You've spent years practising the opposite.

Mindful Seeing

This one might be excruciatingly difficult. Try to see something without doing a million other things, outside or inside your head.

Go to a beautiful spot and see the beauty. No selfies. Notice when you get lost in thoughts. Bring your awareness back to what you see.

Try watching a TV show or a movie and only doing that. Not watching it while studying. Not watching it with your phone in one hand and a slice of pizza in the other. Not watching it while planning emails you'll write as soon as it's done. Can you watch it all the way through without skipping ahead or switching channels or searching for something better? Can you practise not judging the people you're watching?

Mindful Cooking

This one might be my favourite: prepare a meal mindfully. You don't need to put music on or listen to a podcast as you cook. Try to open up all of your senses to the meal you're preparing. Enjoy the food. Recognise all of the work that went into getting it to you. Water and sunshine and the energy of so many people made that food possible. Enjoy that you're preparing that food for yourself or for others. Recognise the work you're doing for you.

If you don't know how to cook, that's OK. I didn't either. I had many compulsions in the kitchen, so cooking was not something I delved into when I struggled with my mental health. But as I took steps to get over mental illness, I saw that I needed to do a lot of work in the kitchen to help my brain. So I took cookery classes. The classes created opportunities to tackle many fears I had about harming myself or others, food poisoning, stoves and being a terrible chef. By learning how to handle and prepare food as I overcame those fears, cooking also became a way to practise mindfulness. Now, the act of cooking each day is a way I can nourish my body while also practising the skills that help me take care of my mental health.

How to Succeed at Mindfulness:

1. Do the thing you're doing
2. Breathe
3. Keep doing the first two steps

STEP 4

Meditate

If life was a sports pitch and mindfulness was the game you played on that pitch, meditation would be the practice drill that improves your capacity to play the game and succeed. Meditation is the focused practice of mindfulness skills. When you start to meditate regularly, it will feel as if you are developing strength and endurance in your head that you can then apply through mindfulness in your everyday life. If you notice yourself struggling to apply mindfulness with specific experiences, meditation provides an opportunity to work on your skills to address those challenges. That's why I've divided mindfulness and meditation into two different steps. It's just like playing football: if you struggled to keep running during matches, you'd run even harder during practice sessions off the field so you'd have greater capacity available to you during a game.

Like any kind of drill to develop a skill, meditation is difficult. You may struggle with it (a lot). Meditation is not a magical panacea that brings instant calm and tranquillity, washing away anxiety and every other emotion you don't like. Meditation is a practice, not a light switch. And it's a practice you need to begin incorporating into your life. It'll take time to make space for it, so get started. I've included it at this point in the book because it's not something to do after you get your mental health and emotions sorted out. Start now, even if it's a struggle.

If you don't meditate, meditation is very difficult and you won't experience any of the benefits of meditating. If you don't practise meditation, it's completely natural to struggle to pay attention, to have difficulty handling emotions or to be incapable of stopping that hamster wheel of thoughts spinning in your head.

If you do meditate, meditation is still difficult and you might experience some benefits eventually. So enjoy the practice of meditation for itself, not for some distant outcome you're craving. Treat it like a friend. Don't bring it into your life only to take from it. If you're selfish with meditation, you will have an unhappy relationship with it.

With meditation – or practising any skill we explore in this book – you can come to enjoy the challenge of bringing that skill into your life. I hope you can discover that the challenges of meditation are also benefits of the practice. They'll bind your friendship together.

MEDITATION IS A HUMAN PRACTICE

Meditation is the oldest 'new thing'. Religions around the world have played an important role in carrying this practice from ancient times into our contemporary era. When I became interested in meditation and wanted to learn more about it, the only groups I could find in my city were all connected to religions. (For some of these groups, calling them 'religions' was a very liberal use of the word. They were cults. But they had *free* meditation classes – with juice and *cookies*!) So I would go to a session and there'd be all of this singing and chanting and reading passages from religious books tacked on to the meditation. (And the cookies were never nice cookies. Nobody feels closer to enlightenment when they're eating nasty cookies.) It took me a long time to find a meditation group that I liked.

The connection to religion can be a barrier for many people when they try to access the benefits of meditation. You might hear about research that shows that meditating for eight weeks can increase grey matter density in areas of your brain associated with memory and learning,[8] or that long-term meditators exhibit more grey matter in areas associated with sensory awareness and executive decision-making when compared to people who do not meditate,[9] or that it supports people in being less emotionally triggered,[10] or that it helps you keep your mind from wandering off when writing tests,[11] and you might think, Wow, I want some of that! But then you find the closest meditation group, and the guy at the front of the room starts talking about having three eyes and past lives and aligning his chakras, and you quickly line up your chakras straight out of the door.

Meditation is a fundamentally human practice. You sit there, you breathe, you be. It's a focused, intentional practice of being mindful of being. It strips away everything except existence. It's as human as you can get.

Religion can be part of that or not. When I'm talking about meditation or mindfulness throughout this book, I'm talking about them as actions that anybody can practise. Religion need not be attached to the exercise of meditation any more than it need be attached to any other exercise. Whether you pray or swear before doing deadlifts or cardio is entirely up to you. The same goes for meditation.

There's a chapter coming up later on non-judgement (see page 199), and if you feel an urge to dismiss meditation simply because it's been associated with religion or a religion that you don't practise, then I'd suggest you get a head-start on practising non-judgement. My judgements were a barrier to getting started with meditation at first. The group I attend at the moment is led by a teacher, Ronit Jinich, who practises in the tradition of the Zen teacher Thich Nhat Hanh. There are certainly many aspects of the practice that are Buddhist, but I am not Buddhist, nor do I need to be to find value in stopping, sitting and breathing with my neighbours. I sometimes make cookies to bring to class.

I STRUGGLE WITH MEDITATION

That struggle is useful. It helps me learn how to meditate. My unruly puppy mind constantly wants to run around, chase after every stick my brain throws for it and find inappropriate places to stick its nose. Even when my mind does come back to me in the present, it's usually dragging something dead and messy it's dug up from the past.

Learning how to get my mind to sit and breathe with me has been a long and useful journey. From years of training, my mind has learned always to run off into the past or the future to look for the next uncertainty to throw at me. Finding time for meditation is also challenging amidst all of the competing priorities in my life. I'm sure you also have a long list of things you could be doing at any moment, and that list is always growing longer. I hope you learn the benefits of prioritising meditation on that list. It's not something I can convince you to prioritise. If you don't run, it must seem absurd to see people waking up early to go jogging in the cold morning air. If you haven't experienced the benefits of that practice, it's impossible to imagine why somebody would prioritise it. Let's talk more about running as a way to help you get your meditation practice going.

CONSIDER HOW YOU WOULD BECOME A RUNNER

Starting a meditation practice is analogous to starting a running practice. They parallel each other to an uncanny extent, in skills and in outcomes. On top of that, whether you join a meditation group or a running group, at the end of the session, you're guaranteed there'll always be people whingeing about their knees.

If somebody wanted to start running, she would start small, she'd do it with a partner or join a group or get a coach, she'd make time in her life for it, she'd do it consistently if she wanted to see results, she'd make changes in the rest of her life to support her running, and so on. This is all true with meditation as well: no one can convince you to do it; you have to want to practise and make time for it. Using running as an analogy, consider the following as you start your meditation practice:

1. **Start small**
   If you haven't been meditating regularly (or at all) it's totally natural to not have the skills or capacity to meditate for very long. Start with 10 or 15 minutes each day for the first week. Even if you've meditated in the past but have taken a break for many months, you'll find it's difficult again – just as you would find running difficult if you took a break from that for several months.

2. **Stay consistent**
   The ability to pay attention is exactly like your capacity for cardiovascular endurance. If you're not consistently exercising and improving it, then it will decline. If you run a 5K race but then stop training after it, how long would it be before you couldn't run 5K without stopping? Not very long. So plan for the long-term with meditation. It has to become part of your life. Consider how you've made other practices consistent parts of your life – even unhealthy practices. What makes them stick?

3. **Push into the discomfort while acknowledging your limits**
   Start small but challenge yourself. It's OK to struggle with meditation. Find where it's difficult and give yourself permission to struggle. You'll discover where your limits are. Gradually push into them. It might be useful to start with guided meditation audio tracks because they give you something extra to focus on. Try searching online for Jon Kabat-Zinn's recordings for the Mindfulness-based Stress Reduction course. Many people I work with enjoy Andy Puddicombe's work and his Headspace

app. For loving-kindness meditation, which we'll talk about later in this book, Sharon Salzberg has many recordings, and Ronit also has some useful audio guides online that help break down the steps of practising loving-kindness meditation. We'll explore more later about why it's so tough to practise loving yourself. Also try meditating without an audio guide. What challenges arise? How does your mind behave differently? What happens when you sit for a much longer period of time?

4. **Be kind to yourself. Why would you be able to meditate?**
You might be really bad at meditation. Unless there's a special reason you shouldn't be bad at it, expect to struggle at it. That's wonderful! You're on an exciting journey with this practice. If you want to judge yourself or get angry at meditation for not 'working', you can do that, but adding that extra baggage will only make this experience more difficult. How will you enjoy sitting and breathing with your brain if you're also hauling around heavy judgements and big assumptions? Would you expect yourself to run a marathon a month after you started running as a hobby?

5. **Expect the unexpected**
If you were new to running, you'd experience aches and pains and pleasurable sensations and all sorts of fascinating side-effects. Shin splints? Higher libido? Who knows what might happen?! You've never used your body like that before and, if you're new to meditation, you've never used your mind like this before. Whatever experiences you have will be awesome experiences to have while meditating. You can be mindful of those emotions, thoughts or physical sensations. That *is* the practice. Invite them to sit beside you while you breathe. Let them pile on top of you. Let them run away on their own. You don't have to judge them or yourself for experiencing them. You don't have to get rid of them. Can you be willing to let them be?

6. **Make time**
    I don't meditate at the same time every day. I also don't exercise at the same time every day. Some days line up and others don't. My schedule is constantly changing. What's important is that I set aside time to meditate. In the morning, I figure out a time to meditate and then I defend that time. It would be easy to think of a million reasons why I'm too busy today and can always do extra meditation tomorrow to make up for it. But that meeting with my breath is something I respect as I would any other meeting. I can't reschedule a meeting with such an important partner. It might be the most important meeting I have all day.

7. **Explore the practice**
    One of the benefits to adopting such an ancient practice is that you can support yourself with an immense array of books, videos, audio tracks, apps, scrolls and even stone tablets. You don't have to meditate in a vacuum. Explore different types of meditation. Read about meditation in books written by people who died centuries ago. Any challenge that you run into is a challenge that somebody else has already encountered and written a book about. Dive into that wealth of wisdom.

8. **Connect with other people**
    A great way to support your meditation practice is to connect with others. It's like joining a running group – it can help with consistency and overcoming challenges along the way. You don't even need to do it in-person if there's no group in your area. Connect with people online who share similar meditation goals and practices. Finding meditation buddies can help to remind you to meditate, and you can discuss how to overcome challenges together.

9. **Modify your practice to fit your context**
    Not everybody runs in the same way. Some like trail running, others like obstacle races; some hit the treadmill at the gym

or run as part of triathlons, others ditch running in favour of skiing or swimming or racing wheelchairs. However, common to all of them is that they're building endurance and strength by pushing their limits. There are many types of meditation. Explore what works for you. Try not to get caught up in the superficial characteristics of meditation. If you can't sit cross-legged on the floor, don't. Find a way to practise that's comfortable for you within your context.

10. Set goals that rocks can't do better than you

As with anything related to mental health, don't forget this fundamental principle. I find it useful to set goals that are entirely in my control. I control for how long I meditate each day. That's about it. I don't control what pops into my head or what happens around me while I meditate. I don't control any feelings I might have while I meditate. I don't control any long-term outcomes of meditating. I only control paying attention to my next breath. How long will you meditate each day?

BUT WHAT IF I TRIED MEDITATION AND IT DIDN'T WORK?

Telling somebody that you tried meditation and it didn't work is like telling somebody that you tried weightlifting and it didn't work. Either you didn't do it consistently for long enough, you were trying to get something out of it that it doesn't provide, you were putting more practice into skills that make your health worse, or you were doing some combination of all of the above.

Meditation works. It's very easy to get it to work for you. All you need to do is meditate and you've successfully reached the goal of meditation, which is: to meditate. You're successful at it if you're doing it. There is nothing else to pursue.

When people encounter barriers with meditation, they're

typically struggling with the concepts we covered at the beginning of the book. So, they're not approaching mental health and emotional fitness as practices; they're trying to be like a rock that doesn't feel or think; and they're trying to relieve symptoms instead of tackling problems. Let's look at how the concepts from the previous chapters apply in your meditation practice.

Barrier 1: Not approaching mental health and emotional fitness as practices

In the Introduction we looked at how emotional fitness is like cardiovascular fitness: you push into difficult experiences, and you keep going. Through that regular practice, your endurance, flexibility and strength improve. Emotional fitness, like cardiovascular fitness, isn't something you can directly change. You have to do regular exercises that push your limits and, through those exercises, your fitness level improves. Meditation is an exercise that can help you push your limits.

When you sit or lie down to breathe in the present, you'll experience feelings, thoughts and physical sensations you don't like. That will give you the opportunity to build your capacity to handle them. Initially, it's highly likely that will be frustrating. Thoughts will pop up about something you regret saying, or you'll feel overwhelmed by physical sensations, or you'll automatically begin reassuring yourself that you're not a stupid, horrible person. You'll have arguments in your head with your ex-boyfriends and current girlfriends. You'll get flooded with emotions you've been covering up. You might spend the entire time worrying about work and then get angry at yourself for 'wasting' your meditation time and being 'bad' at it. All of this is normal. Having stuff in your head, whatever that stuff is, is totally normal. Chasing after it is normal. That's why we start to practise meditation, so we can learn how to bring our awareness back to the present.

As my meditation teacher, Ronit Jinich, often says when we come together in her living room to sit and breathe, 'Practice *is* perfect.' That's what we're there to do. We notice when we start chasing after thoughts and judgements and then we bring our awareness back to the present. That's the exercise: the repetition of bringing our awareness back to the present, like lifting a weight, pedalling a wheel round and round, or jogging one foot after the other on the pavement. And we'll reach our limits, again and again. We won't be able to go any further or lift any more or keep our awareness in the present. So we try again. The practice is bringing our awareness back to the present. Do it again!

Barrier 2: Trying not to feel or think

If you go to a bookstore displaying many meditation or mindfulness-based therapy books, the dominant graphic design motif on those book covers will likely be: rocks. There'll be pictures of smooth rocks stacked on top of each other, or maybe a single rock surrounded by gracefully ridged sand in a Zen garden. But this rock motif is misleading. The purpose of meditation is not to become a rock. If you come to meditation in the hope that it'll help you get rid of feelings or thoughts you don't like and you can become an unfeeling rock, then meditation will only become another compulsion. It will only bring more of those unwanted feelings and experiences into your life.

With meditation, we can learn how to feel completely. We can experience any thought or emotion, without judgement, and explore what it means to have that experience. If you're anxious and you meditate, you'll feel anxious while you meditate. If you struggle with intrusive thoughts, you'll have them when you meditate. That's fine. That's what you're experiencing in the present. Can you become curious about those experiences? Can you welcome them to sit beside you while you meditate? Can you recognise that they're not you, they're experiences?

Barrier 3: Trying to relieve symptoms instead of tackling problems

Meditation is not a replacement for cutting out compulsions, changing unhelpful beliefs, or changing the systems around you that are causing you distress. If you started to meditate because you wanted to relieve painful symptoms of that monster chewing on you, then you're right back in that example I talked about earlier, taking painkillers while the monster eats you alive. Meditation isn't something you tack on to an unhealthy life and expect it to magically transform that life. Meditation is not a quick fix to problems in your life. It is also not a long fix to problems in your life. Meditation helps you practise skills and build capacity to accept the stuff in your head while making healthy decisions in the present. It can help you practise handling internal experiences you don't like so you can improve your ability to make changes in your life, but you still have to make those changes, whether they're in things you're doing or with things happening to you. If you start meditating because you're stressed at work, either because you work in an unhealthy environment or engage in behaviours at work that make it very stressful for you, don't expect meditation to change that. You'll just be a person who works in an unhealthy environment who also meditates, or a person who procrastinates all the time who also happens to meditate (if you do manage to get round to doing that). So make changes. Practise meditation to build your capacity to make those changes.

*

Now you can put all of this together simply by trying meditation. Whatever happens, happens. The exercise I share here is a very basic meditation practice that will help you begin to explore the fundamentals of meditation, and you might have an opportunity to experience some of the barriers we have just discussed. Later meditation exercises in the book will build on this basic exercise, so be sure to try it out a couple of times if you're new to meditation.

EXERCISE: **Meditation**

Even with 10 minutes of sitting and breathing, you can practise that fundamental skill of having an experience and making a choice aligned with your values.

For this basic exercise, you're going to sit, close your eyes, and practise bringing your awareness to your breath for about 10 minutes. If you're listening to the audio version of this book while you're driving or jogging, please don't close your eyes. Keep driving or jogging (with your eyes open). You can try this exercise later when you're not moving.

1. Set a timer for 10 minutes.
2. Grab a seat and get comfortable.
3. When you're ready, hit start on the timer.
4. Gently close your eyes and then bring your awareness to where you're in contact with whatever it is you're sitting on. Notice the physical sensation of contact and let that pin down your chattering mind for a moment. Be with that awareness of touch for several breaths.
5. Then slowly bring your awareness up your body. Take a couple of breaths at each body part. Say hello to each one. Smile at a knee, wave to your belly button. Notice the posture of your body as you bring your awareness up to your chest moving in and out as you breathe.
6. Breathe normally. Your body is an expert at breathing. You're simply bringing your awareness to your breath as it moves in and out of your body, raising your chest up and down.
7. Spend some time like this, simply aware of being and breathing. Slow down. Get your brain to sit with you. Keep your awareness with each inhale and each exhale.

8. While you're doing this, you might find it helps you to focus if you count each inhale and each exhale, up to 10. You breathe in. That's one. You breathe out. That's two. When you reach 10 start over. This isn't about seeing how long you can hold your focus. If 10 is too high, start with four or even two. Notice a breath in and notice a breath out. Repeat.
9. Your brain will throw some thoughts at you and you might notice you start to chase after them or judge them. That's OK. Gently bring your awareness back to your breath. That's what we're practising here: noticing when our awareness has wandered off and then bringing it back. It's like flexing a muscle. That's all we're doing for 10 minutes.
10. When the timer goes off, gently bring your awareness back to the room around you. Notice the sound of the timer. Notice your posture. Come back to that sensation of contact where you began. And then turn off the timer.

Here's something to consider. When I first began to practise meditation, my thoughts would race incredibly quickly, as if the hamster wheel up in my head was being spun by a hamster on steroids. It could take me 10 minutes simply to quieten my mind. This exercise might be similarly difficult for you. It may seem like 10 minutes of struggle. That's normal. Keep practising *and* try meditating for longer. Those first 10 minutes can be like warming up to run – at first your legs are stiff and sore and it won't feel like a good day to exercise. But it is a good day to exercise! Your brain just doesn't know it yet.

STEP 5

Follow your values

> 'One of the things that helped me a lot with my mental health is the decision I made that I prefer spending my time doing the things I love rather than spending it on trying to figure out what thoughts are part of my mental health challenges. I just let them come and go, while I live my life the way I want to live it.'
>
> Diana

Before we get to the chapters about cutting out compulsions that fuel poor mental health, we need to talk about values. We'll come back to values constantly throughout the rest of the book. We build better mental health on our values. Values are the directions we want to move in with each step we take in our lives. Through the Inventory exercises we covered earlier, you can see your values in your Ideal Inventory, and can recognise how your actions are misaligned with your values when you see things on the present Inventory you're not happy about.

    Values are at a level above goals. Goals tell you what you want, but values tell you *why* you want it. For example, you might value friendship. With a value like that, you can ask yourself: 'How do I build friendships?' You might decide to build them by creating opportunities in your hectic schedule to see your friends and support them. That awareness could translate into a specific goal, such as: 'I'll organise a time to hang out with my friends at least once every week.'

Use your values as a compass on the journey ahead. They'll help you understand which direction to go in when you encounter uncertainty. Once you understand the direction to go, you can set goals that align with that direction and then you can take action.

The importance of values is something I learned when I started therapy and began to cut out compulsions. But I didn't actually learn it during therapy sessions – I learned it in the tech sector.

Exposure and Response Prevention (ERP) therapy basically involves cutting out the compulsions you would normally engage in when anxious. I'd practised trying to avoid anxiety my entire life, so my compulsions had become automatic reflexes. It took me more than a week of sweating through excuses and anxious failures before I succeeded for the first time at not checking the front door lock after locking it on my way out. And that was only the first compulsion I tried to tackle. I had so many others to cut out.

At the same time that I was doing ERP therapy with Dr Whittal, I also happened to be in graduate school, and had the opportunity to collaborate with Tom Wujec. Tom is a designer and author; he's given several popular TED talks, he's a Fellow at Autodesk, a software engineering pioneer, and he facilitates visual thinking workshops with organisations around the world to help them innovate and find clarity in complex situations. Often at the start of workshops, Tom would draw a diagram like this:

That is the Unhappiness Curve. The 'T' is for time and the 'U' is for unhappiness. When any person or group innovates – when they attempt to do something new – they start up the Unhappiness Curve. They experience a drastic increase in feelings they don't like. Uncertainty begins to rise, people worry about what will happen, they're afraid they might lose their job, the company will fail, they'll get blamed, etc. The pressure increases to fall back on what they've done before, what's safe, what they know.

[Graph: curve of u vs t, bell-shaped rising then falling]

If they give in to that pressure, they drop off the curve and go back to what they were doing before (see the diagram below). Unhappiness goes away, but they don't innovate. The change they wanted to create doesn't happen. They make a short-term decision to relieve their anxiety at the long-term expense of the health and well-being of the organisation.

[Graph: same curve with arrow showing drop back to "WHAT YOU'VE DONE BEFORE"]

I realised that that was what I was doing every time I tried to cut out a compulsion but failed. I would experience more and more feelings I didn't like, I'd fall back on what I'd done before, and I'd experience temporary relief. But my company was failing. I was not meeting the needs of my number 1 customer: me.

In Tom's workshops, much of the work would then focus on exploring what the organisation, or its customers, actually valued. The group could then use those values to pull themselves up and over the Unhappiness Curve. Values help a team say: 'OK, we're all upset and confused right now. That's normal. But these values reflect what our customers want. We need to change to do what our customers want, regardless of what we're comfortable with or what we've done before.' When organisations can accept their internal experiences and stick to what they value, or what their customers value, innovation and change happens.

For you, that means accepting that you're anxious or scared, but instead of reacting to that with a decision aimed at short-term relief, you push through that feeling and do what's best and healthiest for the long term.

Although the process of cutting out a compulsion is simple to explain — you accept the stuff in your head and you do something you value, instead of reacting to that stuff with coping, checking or controlling compulsions — the practice is much more challenging. Values will help pull you through.

When you're mired in uncertainty, values empower you to take a step that contributes to being healthy and happy over the long term.

Your values empower you to say things like, 'OK, I'm experiencing the urge to go through my partner's social media channels right now to see if he's chatting with anybody that's better looking than me, but what I'll do is put my phone down and make myself breakfast because I value taking care of my health. I don't value investing my time and energy in making myself miserable, jealous and paranoid.'

Because so much of the struggle with our mental health is about trying to avoid uncertainty and move away from experiences, it's normal for that struggle to send us way off course in life. Fear becomes the fuel for our actions. And then our actions are all about things we don't care about. If you give up control of your life to fear and you're not doing things you care about, it's totally normal to sink deep into depression and anxiety. You're being somebody you never wanted to be.

Values are what matters to you. Struggling with mental health is all about pouring your time and energy into things that *don't* matter to you. Building better mental health is all about investing your time and energy in things that *do* matter to you.

DRIVING DANGEROUSLY AWAY FROM FEAR

I grew up in the countryside of southern Ontario, Canada. It's all fields and forests and small towns. Hockey is popular. Ginseng farms are replacing the old tobacco farms. The sunsets are astounding. The night sky is plastered with stars.

My family lived in a house that was equidistant between two small towns, Norwich and Burford. I went to high school in Burford but also had some friends in Norwich. One year, some of my friends from Norwich invited me to attend their prom, the big end-of-year formal dance at their school. I was a replacement date for a friend of a friend, so this wasn't a big date with my high-school sweetheart. This was only about having a good time.

I went to a friend's place in Norwich before it was time to meet the larger group and head to the dance. At some point, while we were waiting at his house, I realised I didn't have my suit jacket with me. I immediately became nauseous. I knew there would be photos, and I was terrified of being the only guy in the photos not wearing a suit jacket. People would judge me. I'd be the weird guy that didn't know how to dress properly.

I had to get that suit jacket. But my home was a 15-minute drive away, and then I'd have to drive another 15 minutes to get back to Norwich. I didn't want to be late meeting everybody. What would people think if I made the entire group late?! I decided my only option was to drive back and get the jacket. And, if I had to make the trip, there was only one variable I could control: speed.

I drove way above the speed limit the entire way. It was a straight road – a relatively major road in the area – but with some hills. Had any person or puppy been on the other side of one of those hills as I flew over them, I'd have had no chance of stopping before hitting them. I drove faster than I'd ever driven before in my life. I was speeding so much and was so oblivious to my surroundings that I didn't notice my father's car, just outside Norwich, driving in the opposite direction to bring me my suit jacket (mobile phones were still rare then). He turned around to follow me but I was going so fast that he only caught up when I was a minute away from our house and I slowed down for a turn.

That race to get a jacket haunted me for many years. As I dug the mental illness hole deeper, my anxiety about driving increased. Memories of that drive would leap into my consciousness at random moments and it would be as if I was right back there. I'd feel the anxiety and adrenaline again. The fact that I could have hit somebody or had an accident made it seem like I *had* had an accident. What if I actually had hit a little kid playing in the ditch by the side of the road and I'd kept on driving without noticing? Maybe the parents only discovered what had happened an hour or two later when their child didn't come home for dinner? I knew I hadn't been paying attention on the race home. For years I was certain there was an ongoing police manhunt for me. Every time that memory popped into my head, my stomach was devoured by a gang of vicious moths.

I no longer struggle with anxiety about driving, or intrusive thoughts about accidentally killing people, or getting arrested – and in the chapters to come we'll explore what was involved with getting over those obsessions – but now when I look back on the experience, it's such a useful reminder of why values are important, and how making decisions based on fear can take us away from who we are. Let's assume that I had hit a kid that night ...

The Ministry of Transportation might count it as a 'traffic accident' or a 'road fatality involving pedestrian', but was it accidental? I chose to be on that road, driving the way I was driving. I didn't mean to kill anybody, but I didn't mean to drive well or safely. I only wanted to get home as quickly as possible to avoid my fear of being judged for what I was (not) wearing.

Were my actions at that time aligned with what I valued in life? Was attending school dances a life goal of mine? Not at all. Did I love suit jackets? Nope. I was driving like that because I didn't want to feel embarrassed. I was trying to prevent that fear from coming true. But if you'd asked me that day what I cared about in life, would I have said my goal in life was to avoid embarrassment? No.

How cheap am I that I would throw myself away for a fear?

In so many ways, this happens constantly in our lives. We want to be in loving relationships, but push people away because our time and energy is pumped into chasing titles and trophies to avoid feeling worthless. We want to be healthy, but stay up all night making ourselves exhausted while we research illness symptoms because we're afraid we're about to die. We want to spend our working hours helping others, but our fears about money keep us locked into jobs we hate, making excuses for why the harm we cause others is a necessary evil. We want to enjoy hobbies we're passionate about, but instead spend our free time chasing addictions to control feelings we haven't learned to handle.

Are you in charge of how you spend your time and energy each moment of the day? Or is fear in charge? Because if fear is in charge, it's going to take you to that place you never wanted to be, doing things you never wanted to do. When we put values in charge of our actions, we can move towards the places we've always wanted to go and do the things we've always wanted to do.

WHAT MATTERS TO YOU?

In the previous chapters, we went over skills (such as mindfulness) and concepts (such as the fact that you are not a rock) to help you practise accepting internal experiences. Once you're practising acceptance, acting according to your values is the movement that completes this healthy exercise. Acting according to your values is what you'll choose to do instead of following coping, checking and controlling compulsions. That's the practice of being yourself.

What initially got me thinking that I might be struggling with my mental health was noticing I couldn't do the things that mattered to me anymore. There was a gap between the person I knew I was and the person I was acting as.

I had moved to a new city, and with some money I'd saved up I decided to take some time off to write a novel. It's what I'd always said I wanted to do and now I had the ideal opportunity to do it. I spent about six months trying to write that book. I got nowhere because I was spending more and more time on my compulsions. There were so many anxieties and feelings and uncertainties to react to, I didn't have time for writing.

You might have noticed a similar tension in your life, between who you know you are and who you're acting as. It's incredibly exhausting to be more than one person. Sometimes we're acting as many different people in different areas of our lives. It's only natural that trying to be somebody you're not creates anxiety and depression.

Mental health is the practice of being yourself. Improving your emotional fitness enables that practice so you can feel whatever you feel while being yourself. That can be frightening sometimes.

You might get rejected. You might make somebody angry. You might make many people reject you angrily. But if you're acting as yourself, you can handle whatever happens. There is strength in aligning your identity and your actions. If you pretend to be somebody that you're not, and you need to maintain two selves, then those two selves can only ever be half as strong as the single, aligned self (although they'll probably be much weaker because of all the energy you'll waste running back and forth between your different selves, trying to remember all of the lies you need to maintain, dealing with the frustration of becoming incredibly skilled at being somebody you're not).

If somebody looked at how you currently spend your time and energy, and they defined you based on that, would you be happy with their definition of you?

When you looked at the results of the Inventory exercise (page 34), did you see yourself? Or did you see a whole lot of time and energy being spent on somebody you never wanted to be? What do you need to value to bridge the gap between the Inventory and the Ideal Inventory? What matters to you in life? If you were completely you, what would your life look like?

EXERCISE: Setting Values

This exercise is very simple: articulate your values.

Write your values down or draw them or type them up in a place you can easily access. Make sure you can edit them – they'll evolve. Here are some tips for setting values:

1. Your values don't have to be right or perfect. They're directions that help guide you when you take steps in each moment of your life. As you take those steps, you may see that the consequences aren't moving you in the direction you want to walk in life. So modify your values.

2. Values help you make tough decisions in the present that contribute to health and happiness over the long term. They're not there to make you feel good. Learning how to experience sadness, loss, pain, suffering, anger and the entire range of emotions we experience is very useful for health and happiness. So don't pursue masking compulsions as values. If you want to value not feeling anxiety or not being wrong, or anything that involves not feeling or thinking something, you're screwed.
3. Values translate into actions. Try to go beyond adjectives. A sunset is nice. You're nice. But what do you do? You might use a broad descriptor for a value but make sure you know what specific actions that term translates into on a daily basis.
4. Values aren't an excuse to judge yourself and engage in more compulsions. If you recognise that you didn't act in line with your values, be mindful of that. It happened. You're probably experiencing the natural consequences of that step off your path, which is why you're aware of it. But it's in the past now. What matters is that the next step you take is towards the direction you want to move in life.
5. Values adapt easily to different situations. If you notice yourself getting overly specific, consider why you value that specific thing. Do you value getting promoted at work? Or is that simply a goal that's aligned with your value of taking care of your family, and you see promotion as a means by which you can achieve this? If that's the case, then I'd suggest not getting too attached to the promotion. At this moment, that might be a way that you can take care of your family, but as the context around you changes, better ways to do this may present themselves. You don't want to be blindly pursuing that

promotion if the company is failing or if they ask you to do things that take you away from your family. If we pursue a tactic or a goal, we can miss the things we actually value.

MENTAL HEALTH IS THE PRACTICE OF BEING YOURSELF

STEP 6

Focus on changing actions, not thoughts or feelings

'When facing difficult situations, I realised that saying "I can't" usually means I don't want to do something because of the possibility of experiencing a particular feeling or result I might not like. So if I want to move forward and past challenges, then I have to decide if experiencing and learning how to deal with these feelings and uncertainties is something I'm willing to do.'

Kianni

If you want to improve your mental health, it helps if you're not investing heavily in making your mental health worse. As we explored in the chapter on mindfulness, if you practise distracting yourself for several hours every day, it's only natural that you become very skilled at being distracted. It's the same with physical fitness. If you exercise for 30 minutes a few times each week but spend several hours every night watching television, eating junk food and smoking, the investment in exercise will have negligible returns compared to the investment in everything that's damaging your body. Hopefully this is not a shocking realisation.

When we want to build better mental health and do more of the things that matter to us in life, it's important that we stop taking steps in the opposite direction. That's why cutting out compulsions is so important. As I've said, compulsions are the coping, checking and controlling we engage in as a reaction to uncertainty, anxiety and other feelings we don't like. The more we engage in the compulsions, the more we have those experiences we don't like. But understanding the connection between the compulsions and their effects isn't always obvious.

Imagine we're in a hot, sunny place. There's a big pool underneath some palm trees, lounge chairs all around it, beautiful hibiscus plants with bright pink flowers. The buzz of cicadas fades into the afternoon heat and the clink of ice in glasses dances through the air as you close your eyes and relax by the pool. At least, you try to relax, but it's difficult because there's this guy running around the pool shouting.

He yells out: 'I love jumping in the water!' And then he cannonballs into the pool. A big splash throws water on everybody around. Immediately, he pulls himself out of the pool, shouting angrily: 'I hate getting wet! Why does this always happen to me?! All I wanted to do was jump in the water! I didn't ask to get wet!'

He grabs a towel and furiously dries himself off, muttering about how terrible he feels. 'If only there was something I could do to get rid of this nasty feeling. It doesn't feel right. I wish I felt like I did when I was getting ready to jump in the pool. I was so happy. Being wet just isn't me. I'm not my normal, dry self now. I wish there was something I could do so I didn't feel like this anymore. I should really do something I enjoy, something for me, like jumping in the pool. I love that feel of jumping in the pool. Things feel right when I'm jumping.'

He runs a lap around the pool and belly flops off the diving board with a wet *smack*.

He heaves himself back out of the pool again, growling, 'Everything I love always gets ruined!'

This pattern will repeat itself until he's used up all the towels, or he knocks himself unconscious diving into the shallow end, or somebody locks him in the pool house, or he simply wastes the rest of his life running in circles, jumping in the water, hating how he feels, trying to get rid of that feeling, jumping in again, and then hating how he feels, again.

That was me when I struggled with my mental health.

Jumping in the water and getting wet are not separate. Liking compulsions but hating the outcomes is no less absurd than somebody who likes jumping in the water but hates getting wet. They need to stop jumping in the pool.

While it's easy to spot the connection between jumping in the water and getting wet, it might not seem so obvious when it comes to dealing with the compulsions that are dumping you in the deep end of life. To make those connections, it's helpful to identify patterns of thinking and behaving that aren't helping you in life. It's how and why you do or use something that creates the problems.

SIMPLE PATTERNS OF THINKING AND BEHAVING

I don't talk much about specific mental illness diagnoses because I don't find them particularly useful or scientific. For example, if you're afraid of people disliking you and meeting new people makes you anxious, and you try to control that anxiety by avoiding social situations, if you went to a doctor for help with that, the doctor might diagnose you with Social Anxiety Disorder.

But if your reaction to that anxiety about being disliked is to compulsively clean yourself because you believe you could pass on a disease to somebody and kill them and then everybody would hate you, you'd probably get diagnosed with Obsessive Compulsive Disorder. If, however, your reaction to that same anxiety is to get drunk in social situations and you always need to be drunk before getting into any intimate situation with another person because you're afraid of rejection, then you'd probably get diagnosed with the euphemistic-sounding Alcohol Use Disorder. Or if you try to control your anxiety about being disliked by engaging in restrictive eating compulsions because you think controlling your weight is a way to control what others think about you, then you'd probably get diagnosed with an eating disorder.

Mental illness diagnoses are based on superficially identifiable or self-reported symptoms. If we did that with physical illnesses, when you were suffering from pneumonia you'd walk out of the doctor's with diagnoses of Leaky Nose Disease, Coughing Syndrome, Muscle Ache Disorder and Body Temperature Dysregulation Disability. Your doctor could give you medication to reduce the symptoms of all four of those, but that might not do anything about the monster chewing on you: the infection in your lungs.

In those examples of diagnoses I mentioned above, it's the exact same behaviour each time: experiencing uncertainty and feelings you don't like (in this case, related to being disliked by other people); wanting to escape these feelings, to find 'peace of mind', chase certainty, etc.; and then engaging in compulsions to pursue those desires.

We want to look at what brought on those feelings you don't like. So we'll take this system back a bit further, to the experiences we have and the judgements we make about those experiences that lead to the uncertainty, anxiety and other feelings we don't like:

INTERNAL AND EXTERNAL EXPERIENCES → JUDGEMENTS → UNCERTAINTY, ANXIETY, AND OTHER FEELINGS YOU DON'T LIKE → DESIRES → COPING, CHECKING, CONTROLLING

You start by having an experience. Let's say it's an internal experience, for example a memory pops into your head about a time when another kid at school mocked you for making a mistake when you were reading in class. You judge that memory as meaning something about you. You judge yourself as somebody who always makes mistakes when you're stressed. You judge being judged as a very bad thing. That makes you anxious. It just so happens that today you're giving a presentation at work that you don't feel prepared to give. You're uncertain about whether you can do it well, whether people will judge you negatively. You want people to think good things about you. You want to avoid mistakes and embarrassment. So you start on your usual compulsions to pursue those desires and eliminate those feelings you don't like.

The specific experiences, feelings or compulsions *do not matter*. You can fill in the blanks with *any* internal experience and *any* compulsion. We'll come back to this system and when you're cutting out compulsions with the exercises coming up later, map out compulsions using this system to see opportunities for change. Recognise the experiences you're having. See the judgements you're making. Identify the uncertainties you're trying to eliminate. Understand the compulsions you engage in as a reaction to all of that.

To help with understanding the compulsive patterns of behaviour and thinking, I approach them as three overlapping categories. I'll give an overview of them below and then we'll explore each one in depth in the steps ahead.

COPING, CHECKING AND CONTROLLING

When I struggled with mental illness, it seemed as if I had so many compulsions – checking door locks, Googling disease symptoms, not touching raw meat, checking for text messages, unplugging appliances, binge eating, holding knives over the counter so I wouldn't stab somebody, rereading emails over and over again to look for errors, lying to people to try to control what they thought about me, avoiding people, needing to have everything 'right' before I could start working or studying, repeatedly washing my hands to get rid of germs, and the list went on. It might seem daunting to deal with so many compulsions but actually I didn't have millions of them. I only had three.

Coping, checking and controlling are patterns of thinking and behaving. It doesn't matter what the compulsions look like superficially. They can happen entirely inside your head or entirely outside your head. They can affect only you or they can affect other people. They can be things you think of as 'good' or 'bad'. Let's take a look at these three patterns:

1. **Coping** is all about trying to replace feelings or thoughts that you don't like. It's like trying to do yoga to calm yourself down when a hippo is attacking you. Many things we use to cope might seem 'healthy', while others, like drugs or alcohol or junk food, are generally recognised as not so healthy. But the pattern is the problem. If my response to feeling bad is always to make myself feel good, what am I teaching my brain about how to make me feel good? That I need to feel bad first. Coping behaviours reward our brains for experiences we hate.
2. **Checking** is about trying to eliminate uncertainty. Many of us spend all day training our brains to check. It's very easy to check things in our connected world. You can open a dating app to quickly check if somebody likes you. You can send a message to a friend after a drunken night out to check if she's

angry with you. You can post pictures and videos online to check if people think you're attractive. You can instantly check your bank account to make sure that dodgy store you went to didn't overcharge you. You can watch your home online. You can post questions on forums to get reassurance from thousands of people. You can check page after page of information about symptoms to make sure you don't have a deadly disease, or that you're not going insane. You can check the news. You can check unending streams of analytical data about who's doing what, where, whenever. With all of this checking, it's no wonder our brains keep giving us more uncertainties to check.

3. **Controlling** is all about trying to prevent experiences we don't like. Unfortunately, in the process of trying to control things, we actually cause those experiences (or even worse experiences) to happen. Lying and manipulating what we tell others is a very common way this exhibits itself. Lying to make people like us typically leads to them not liking us. We often try to control others to relieve our own uncertainties. You can see this in any group when one member tries to control the others as a reaction to the fear of failure, or when parents hover over their children to relieve uncertainties about the children getting hurt (and the parents getting blamed for being bad parents), or with romantic partners trying to control each other to relieve their anxieties about not being adequate. Controlling is also at work in compulsions that involve violence, in all forms, against ourselves or others.

Now that we've gone over the three types of compulsion, it's time to identify the ones in your life that you want to cut out. We'll use the next exercise to do that. It will help you see the steps you'll take in the weeks ahead to get from where you are right now, to where you want to be.

EXERCISE: The Hierarchy

This is a classic Exposure and Response Prevention (ERP) exercise. A Hierarchy is a ranked list of compulsions. It's an effective tool because it helps to overcome a common challenge people run into when cutting out compulsions: they start with compulsions they don't yet have the skills or emotional fitness capacity to cut out.

For instance, a woman who is struggling with commitment issues might go to a therapist and ask for help to learn how to stop ditching her romantic partners. To her, that seems like the behaviour she wants to cut out. She wants to learn how to live with uncertainty about her partner being 'the one'. But as she digs into her reactions to other uncertainties in her life, she might discover that she always jumps from one career to another at the first sign of difficulty, she often changes plans or cancels things at the last minute, she won't go to a restaurant without researching the menu in advance to make her selection, and that she can spend an hour trying to decide between two different brands of identical cough medicine.

Although a recent relationship experience might be creating significant amounts of anxiety or regret, reacting to uncertainty about choices and commitments is common throughout her life, not only in relationships. If she wants to handle that uncertainty about long-term relationships, she'll benefit from first learning how to cut out compulsions around relatively small choices, such as picking something from a menu or finishing a project at work.

The Hierarchy helps us lay out all our compulsions so we can see the path from where we are to where we want to be. You can do this exercise on paper or with sticky notes, or you can do it using a spreadsheet to make it easy to move the items around as you rank them. Here's how you do the Hierarchy:

Focus on changing actions, not thoughts or feelings

1. Make a list of all the compulsions you engage in to cope with, check on or control uncertainty, anxiety and other feelings you don't like.

   - Refer back to the Inventory exercise (page 34) if you need a reminder of how you're spending your time.
   - Be specific. Something like 'compulsions at work' is too vague. Articulate each of the compulsions at work, i.e.: 'avoiding my boss, using "Reply All" unnecessarily, procrastinating on social media, lying to customers, etc.'

2. Rank the compulsions based on how difficult you think it would be to cut them out. You could give the most difficult a 10, the easiest a 1, and rank the others accordingly.

   - You'll have many compulsions of equivalent difficulty.
   - If you're stuck on where to start ranking, pick two at random and ask yourself which would be more difficult to eliminate. Imagine the practical changes involved and how much anxiety you would experience if you couldn't do that action ever again. Continue with that ranking process until you've sorted through the heap of compulsions.

3. Start working through the compulsions, cutting out one each week, starting with the easiest and working your way up.

4. It's also useful to look at your Ideal Inventory and create a Reverse Hierarchy – a ranked list of all the things you want to do more of in your life. As you cut out one compulsion each week, you can also add one activity you want to do more of in life.

As we progress through the following steps on coping, checking and controlling, you'll learn specific ways to support yourself through the process of cutting out those compulsions and doing more of what matters to you.

Here's an example of what a Hierarchy can look like:

DIFFICULTY	COMPULSION
10	Checking the stove.
8	Not driving.
8	Avoiding touching 'contaminated' things.
7	Leaving my home messy so I have an excuse to not invite people over.
7	Not cooking for others / not giving them food.
7	Checking myself in every reflective surface I pass.
7	Washing until I feel clean.
6	Lying about what I like or dislike.
6	Ending every relationship the moment I think something is wrong.
6	Only eating frozen food / not touching raw meat.
5	Not asking people for things I want.
5	Not leaving social events when I want to because I'm afraid of what people will think or say about me.
5	Boredom binge eating.
4	Saving every receipt.
4	Staying up for hours online instead of going to bed.
4	Checking my lock at the gym / stopping workout early to check locker.
3	Avoiding responsibility at work so I can criticise whoever does take responsibility.
3	Avoiding bills / finances.
3	Not writing emails until I feel 'ready' to write them.

2	Procrastinating on chores.
2	Rewriting and rereading emails.
1	Stalking social media profiles of people I like.
1	Checking door / window locks.

With that Hierarchy example, I would start with the lock-checking compulsions at the bottom and then work my way up, cutting out one compulsion or a set of related compulsions each week. Keep in mind that this example is probably a bit on the short side. You'll probably have more compulsions, but don't get hung up on trying to figure them all out before you get started. You'll discover things to add to your Hierarchy as you move through it. You'll adjust your rankings as you run into challenges.

INSTEAD OF CHANGING THE SYSTEMS THAT MAKE US MISERABLE, WE PROMOTE BRIEF MOMENTS OF SEDATION TO MAKE THEM TOLERABLE

STEP 7

Stop coping

It's easy to teach a puppy to pee on your sofa: give it a biscuit every time it pees on the sofa. Even better, only take it out for a run after it's peed on the sofa. You don't like it when your puppy pees on the sofa? Is that stressful for you? Then don't do things that it likes only after it does things you don't like.

Biscuits are delicious and puppies are poor at setting limits for delicious things, so that puppy will pee on your sofa even when it doesn't necessarily need a biscuit. It likes getting them, long after it's full. So it'll keep peeing on the sofa. It might even pretend to pee on the sofa when there's no pee to pee. Puppies can seem so clever when they want a treat.

Imagine if you only rewarded your brain with things it likes after it does things you dislike. That's exactly what we're doing with coping behaviours. They might make you feel good, but they also send a very clear message to your brain: if you feel something I don't like, I'll give you something you like to get rid of those feelings.

Coping makes unhappiness and illness the prerequisites for happiness and health.

WHAT I'M TALKING ABOUT WHEN I'M TALKING ABOUT COPING

Eliminating coping doesn't necessarily mean cutting out the things we're using or doing to cope. It's important not to conflate the things with the behavioural pattern. Again: it's not the *what* that matters, it's the *how* and the *why*.

When I refer to coping, I'm referring to a pattern of experiencing thoughts or feelings we don't like and then doing something to replace those unwanted experiences with other experiences we think we want. Coping might involve travelling halfway around the world to ride an elephant, or staying at home to watch TV shows all night, or doing yoga, doing heroin, cutting yourself, playing video games, gardening, going shopping, or eating an entire pizza and a pack of cookies – whatever it is that you do to cover up loneliness, sedate your fears, quieten the voice in your head or mask your insecurities.

Yes, I put drugs, yoga, self-harm and elephant-riding in the same category *if* they're attempts to escape feelings, because then they're not different actions. They're the same action: the action of trying to escape feelings.

I'm not suggesting that pattern isn't considered 'normal'. It's arguably the basis for most marketing: feel something bad and buy this thing to feel good again! Beer ads tell you to unwind at the end of a stressful week. Herbal supplements promise to eliminate your stress 'naturally'. Resorts encourage you to 'get away from it all'. Food companies bait you with sweet indulgences as a reward for enduring pain. The message is: get attacked by a monster, buy a new dress to replace the blood-and-guts-stained one, and then everything will be OK.

When you've felt down or sad or stressed or anxious, it's likely you've rewarded your brain. You've tried to unwind, stay 'balanced', relax, mix things up. When your brain feels something you don't like, do you give it a biscuit (figurative or literal)? You're laying out a clear path to rewards, and that path goes straight through stress, poor communication, damaged relationships, hatred, jealousy, self-loathing and peeing on furniture. Instead of changing the systems that make us miserable, we promote brief moments of sedation to make them tolerable.

We need to change those systems.

BUT AREN'T SOME COPING BEHAVIOURS BETTER THAN OTHERS?

As long as we practise compulsive patterns as a reaction to feelings we don't like, we're always in danger of relapse. It's as if you were compulsively hitting yourself in the face with a hammer so we swapped the metal hammer for a soft, inflatable toy hammer. You, however, continued to swing something at your face. Only now, you don't experience the same nasty consequences. That can be an important step to take, so if that's where you're at, that is awesome. It's extremely difficult to take that first step away from old destructive habits. But keep going. You need to eliminate the pattern of behaviour. You need to stop hitting your face.

As long as you swing the compulsion hammer at yourself, even if it's with a 'healthier' hammer, you're stuck in the same old pattern. And when life happens, as it inevitably does, and somebody comes up to you and swaps your soft hammer for a sledgehammer, you're right back to where you were before, and possibly even worse, looking for a way to deal with your smashed up head.

Let stress and anxiety and suffering point you to the problem. They themselves are not the problem. They are symptoms. They're big arrows pointing to whatever it is that needs to change. Sometimes those changes are major shifts in the systems we interact with in society, at school, in relationships, or wherever we may be. Racism, sexism, homophobia, poverty, mental illness stigma – these are all big, systemic problems. They're like crowds of people rushing up to you and smashing you over the head with sledgehammers. We are not responsible for the pain they cause us, but merely coping with that pain cultivates those problems. We need to work with others to change those systems.

At other times, such as when you engage in compulsions, you're creating the pain. That's when you're hitting yourself in the head with the hammer. You don't need painkillers or extra bandages or special mantras to help erase the pain so you can keep smashing yourself in the face. You don't have Bloody Face Personality Disorder. You need to stop swinging hammers at your own feelings.

SO SHOULD I STOP DOING YOGA AND EATING HEALTHILY?

No, that's not what I'm saying. Do them because they're beneficial to your health, not as a reaction to something you don't like. *The activity is not the problem.*

If somebody feels stressed at work and then does drugs to escape that feeling, they're engaging in the same behavioural pattern as somebody that feels stressed at work and then does yoga to escape that feeling. Neither is addressing the source of the stress at work, and it will only grow. Whatever they're doing for relief will eventually stop delivering relief at the same level it did in the past. That is doubly problematic with healthy activities like exercise because you might stop exercising if it stops 'working' or if you no longer feel stressed. Exercise is beneficial to decreasing your risk of disease and early death, regardless of what's happening in your life. On the flip side, being sedentary increases your risk of disease and early death, regardless of whether you like sitting or not.[12]

SO WHAT ARE YOU SUPPOSED TO DO WHEN YOU GET ANXIOUS OR DEPRESSED OR STRESSED?

Feel the emotions. You're human. You have feelings. You have thoughts. You have urges. Once you're experiencing them, they're there. You can experience them, fully, without trying to do anything to them or because of them.

Have you ever been to a Japanese *onsen*? They're baths fed by geothermal water gurgling up from deep in the earth. I lived in Japan for a couple of years and I miss the hot spring baths so much. But I didn't like them at first. They were too hot! Much hotter than any water I had ever touched that wasn't boiling on the stovetop. I wanted to be clean, not poached.

When we dip a foot into anxiety, or guilt, or loneliness, or anger, or any other pool of feelings we've learned to avoid, it's much like somebody taking a hot spring bath for the first time. Alarms go off in our brains – we'll be hurt and damaged if we step deeper into this feeling. Pull your foot out!

Of course, millions of people all over the world love soaking in hot spring baths. Once I learned to not pull my foot back but instead to get in the water – all of the way in – it actually became a very pleasurable experience. Now it's something I look forward to and choose to do. One big difference between hot spring water and the experiences you don't like is that getting into a hot spring bath is a choice. You don't actually have a choice about the experiences you don't like unless you want to get stuck in life. Everything you want to do in life is on the other side of an enormous bath full of thoughts and feelings you've tried to avoid.

This is where the work to build your emotional fitness level comes in. Get naked. Get in. And get soaking. You'll notice this experience will be very physical. You'll experience these feelings or thoughts in the same way you'd feel hot water. It'll be all over your body and your immediate reaction will be to jump out. Let yourself soak in them. You can be you in them. You can enjoy stepping into them and out of them as you move on to doing what you value in life.

ACCEPTANCE & COMMITMENT THERAPY (ACT)

Developed by the professor, researcher, clinical psychologist, author and creator of great metaphors Dr Steven Hayes, ACT is a form of therapy that helps people improve their mental health and embrace experiences by focusing on six core processes: acceptance; cognitive defusion; being present; self as context; values; and committed action. This is all to help people move towards difficult experiences instead of narrowing their world through avoidance. ACT recognises that we create mental health challenges for ourselves by conflating our identity with our thoughts, by rigidly judging our experiences, by trying to avoid those experiences, and by wrapping our lives up in restrictive, unhelpful narratives we tell ourselves about ourselves. The way out of that trap is to ACT:

Accept your reactions and be present.
Choose a valued direction.
Take action.[13]

To fit the language I'm using in this book, and for the purposes of the examples coming up, I'm modifying the wording of the ACT algorithm to:

I accept the stuff in my head and bring my awareness to the present.
I choose a direction aligned with my values.
I take action.

You'll see this format when we go through the examples of cutting out compulsions.

I discovered Dr Hayes' work when I began participating in mental health patient communities online. ACT resonated with me because I'd seen in my own life the effectiveness of these techniques. It also struck me as the personal, therapeutic approach to dealing with the same challenges I was learning to help companies overcome in my work with Tom Wujec. Innovation, whether it's personal or professional, is all about stepping into a hot bath of experiences you don't like and letting your values guide your actions when you want to fall back on what you've done before, even though what you've done before has nearly destroyed you or your company.

Much of what I'm doing throughout this book is melding design thinking and change management tools with an Acceptance and Commitment Therapy approach to handling the stuff in our heads. I can't give you a complete view of ACT (or design thinking) in this book, so I encourage you to continue exploring these practices. They are complex and useful.

THE PRACTICE OF ELIMINATING A COPING COMPULSION

You might not be ready to jump into the hottest water, which is why we did the Hierarchy exercise to figure out the easier compulsions to tackle first (page 84). Begin with something small and work up your capacity to deal with the tougher compulsions. Make it as easy as possible for yourself by starting with something 'normal'. It might be that you always play video games or watch videos before you feel 'ready' to do your work. Maybe you automatically start flipping through social media channels because you don't want to feel bored (even though what you really need to do is your laundry because you're down to your last pair of boxers and you're re-wearing socks you wore last week).

One of the 'normal' coping behaviours I always got caught up in was watching videos online. I'd be stressed or bored and I'd tell myself that if I just watched a couple more music videos or another episode of a Japanese cartoon or maybe a few funny comedy videos then I'd feel better, I would have unwound from the stressful, boring day, I would feel motivated, and then I could accomplish whatever it was I needed to accomplish, even things I didn't want to do. Of course, it never worked out that way. I'd spend the rest of the night watching videos and being angry at myself for not getting anything done that I actually wanted to do.

Using the ACT structure, I'll show you how I approach cutting out coping compulsions like distracting myself online. Here's how I do it:

I accept the stuff in my head and bring my awareness to the present

- I get home after a busy day at work. I need to buy groceries so I can make food for myself for the week, but I don't feel like going to the shop. I want to watch videos. I don't want to do more work.
- The stuff in my head doesn't need to change. My brain can think of reasons to put off going to shop – I'll wake up earlier tomorrow morning and jog there! I've been meaning to start jogging so this is the perfect opportunity! My brain loves to rationalise me into problems. That's OK. Those thoughts can be there. I feel tired and stressed and that's fine, too. Those feelings can be there.
- Watching the videos is the coping compulsion. There's nothing wrong with watching videos.* The problem here is wanting to watch videos to change how I feel before I do something I need to do. I know it's easy to get sucked into the black hole of the internet if I do that. There'll always be one more video I can watch before I feel ready. It could be hours until I feel like going to the shops, if I ever do.

I choose a direction aligned with my values

- Do I value watching kitten videos, or taking care of my health and my finances? Not only will the groceries help me prepare healthy lunches to eat at work, but I'll also save money. If I spend the night watching kitten videos, there's no way that's actually contributing anything to my life that I care about. OK, I might feel good in the short term, but I'll be upset the next day and stressed out and I'll eat some junk food in the windowless basement food court near my office building and then I'll pass out in the afternoon at my desk in a carb-coma, which will make me even more stressed because I'll only end up more behind at work.

* Please watch my online videos (after you get the groceries).

I take action

- I don't watch the videos. Even though it's difficult, I'll choose the action (getting groceries) that will help me move towards my values (being healthy, making smart financial decisions, etc.). I walk out the door, carrying my reusable grocery bag, dragging my screaming brain.
- When I eliminate coping compulsions and align my actions with my values, I'll feel withdrawal symptoms. My brain will thrash around and demand to get fed compulsions. It'll throw thoughts and feelings at me that I don't like. But I don't have to chase after anything my brain throws up. I can practise mindfulness, being present as I get groceries, as I interact with my community, and when I return and prepare food for myself. I can enjoy all of that experience as I act according to my values.

*

You can apply this practice anywhere as you build up your skills. You can see the basics there of building your emotional fitness capacity. Your brain will try to get you to avoid difficult experiences by getting you to do something that feels good but that you don't care about. And you can thank your brain, and take those feelings with you while you head off to do what you value.

You've already got a list of compulsions in your Hierarchy exercise that you can cut out using this ACT approach. Many of the feelings you experience as you work through that list will be intense. You could be doing something like going online constantly to check dating apps and social media sites for messages to reassure yourself that you won't be alone. When you cut out a compulsion like that, you'll come up against that fear of being alone and it can be terrifying. In the chapters coming up we'll look more at how to lift those heavy fears and carry them with us in life. We'll also look at handling other difficult experiences such as sounds, physical sensations, tastes, or visual stimuli that you've developed compulsions around. But right now, to help with any compulsion you're tackling, I'll explain an exercise that's especially helpful if you continually find yourself relapsing into a compulsion you want to cut out.

EXERCISE: Take a Compulsion Journey

This is a design-thinking exercise I first learned from Tom Wujec as a tool to help companies innovate in a way that fits with their customers' lives. When you're doing it with customers, it's often referred to as a 'Customer Journey' or a 'Journey Map', and you map out a current or potential customer's day to understand all sorts of things: why she's not buying from you, how you can help her with challenges she has before or after buying from you, how you can innovate to meet other needs she has, etc.

We'll adapt this exercise to do something very innovative as well: help you cut out compulsions. We'll do that by mapping out everything that happens leading up to a compulsion. By visualising the complete system around it, we'll see opportunities to make changes that might be easier than trying to stop yourself when you're on the verge of a compulsion or deep in it and those addictive loops are already spinning in your head. Here's how it works:

1. Grab something to draw/write with and a piece of paper on which you can draw a complete day. The bigger the paper, the better.
2. Somewhere on the far right side, draw or write the compulsion you're cutting out. It could be any compulsion: drinking booze, watching TV, masturbating to porn, praying, scrolling through social media, doing drugs, binge eating, harming yourself, trolling, knitting, etc.

Stop coping 99

3. From the compulsion, draw a squiggly line around the page. I like to put the compulsion in the bottom right corner and then I draw my squiggly line across the page to the top left corner. Like this:

4. Now, along the squiggly line, draw and write what happened during the day before the compulsion. Here are some events and experiences you might want to illustrate:

a. What did you do right before you started engaging in the compulsion? What were you doing an hour before that?
b. Why were you in the place where you engaged in the compulsion?
c. How did your emotions change throughout the day? What did you feel and when did you feel it?
d. When did you eat? What did you eat?
e. What time did you wake up? How did you feel when you woke up?
f. What unexpected events happened during the day?
g. How did other people affect you?
h. What challenges did you encounter? Did you overcome them? Did they throw you off-course?
i. What worked well? What did you enjoy?

j. What facilitated or enabled the compulsion? Were there other people involved? Did you need equipment to help you do it? If so, what made that equipment accessible?
k. What external social or economic pressures are affecting you?
l. What happened yesterday that affected today?

[Illustration: A day mapped out in a loop — slept in at 7:30am, coffee + donut at desk, STRESS, late project!, procrastinating, morning meeting runs late, 1:30pm Buy Superfood Salad, Happy chatting with my friend, 6:30 train home, turn on computer right away, ME TIME!, 8:30 pizza, lonely, 2:00am]

5. Once the day is completely mapped out, look for where the compulsions actually started. For instance, if you had to pick up alcohol to drink, the compulsion might have started when you convinced yourself you needed to stop by the convenience store that just happens to be beside the shop where you always buy wine. Or maybe the compulsion started when you came home and automatically turned on your computer, as you always do as soon as you walk through the door.

6. That point you identify shows you where you can make changes earlier in the system of your day to prevent yourself getting pushed into a situation where it's more difficult to stop the compulsion. That point may also show you how to predict and prevent relapses. For example, you might see that every time you get drunk, you relapse afterwards, either immediately or the next morning when you're hungover. That doesn't necessarily mean you need to stop drinking, but it shows you where you can proactively bring in supports to help yourself prevent a relapse. That might be as simple as making sure you schedule time with friends the morning after you go drinking so that you're not stuck at home alone with your brain wanting to do whatever compulsions you fall back into.

STEP 8

Break your IF X THEN Y thinking pattern

'Getting better meant that I had to step back from the horror movies that ran on autopilot in my head all day long. I couldn't stop the thoughts and the more I tried the worse they got. This is where mindfulness made the difference. Once I became mindfully aware of the thoughts I placed myself in a position of power – I gave myself a choice as to where I wanted to focus my attention: focus on trying to alleviate the fear or focus on what I needed to do to conquer this hell in my head. Every day I do my best to place myself in that position of power.'

Sophie

There's a simple pattern at work when we're coping, checking and controlling: IF X THEN Y. You could see it back there in the chapter on coping compulsions: IF X (I feel bad) THEN Y (I need to do something to change that feeling). That pattern is at work in all of the compulsive behaviours that fuel poor mental health in our lives. It triggers anger and violence, it's the flimsy foundation that keeps collapsing underneath your sinking self-esteem, and it's the equation that leaves you ruminating for hours and hours. It leads to dependencies, it feeds depression, it's what drives every compulsion you can imagine, physical or mental. It's a very simple, toxic pattern that can consume our lives. It's like running your life on an ancient computer program that produces nothing but errors. In fact, if you've ever learned any computer programming, it's likely that one of the basic techniques you learned early on was the IF-THEN statement. It's a conditional expression in the code that essentially tells the computer: IF a thing matches some criteria, THEN do or don't do some other thing. IF X THEN Y.

This tiny little program in my brain almost crashed my life. It ruled my behaviours. Take a look at the list below and see if you can spot familiar ideas:

IF X THEN Y in action

- IF I leave the stove on, THEN my building will burn down.
- IF I burn down my building, THEN everybody will hate me.
- IF I check the door lock, THEN my kids are safe.
- IF that guy makes eye contact with me, THEN I must be attractive.
- IF I look attractive, THEN I won't die alone.
- IF I get criticised at work, THEN I'll get fired (and have no money and end up on the street homeless and I'll get HIV and I'll be murdered and nobody will like me).
- IF I wash my hands with toxic soap under scalding hot water, THEN they won't have germs on them.
- IF I do mindfulness right, THEN I won't be stressed anymore.
- IF she doesn't respond to my text message immediately, THEN she's having an affair (or she's died in a car accident (or both)).
- IF I think a bad thought, THEN I'm going to hell.
- IF I can't remember what happened, THEN I must have done something terrible.

- IF I don't check my teeth are clean, THEN there'll be something stuck in them and people will think I'm gross and they'll talk about me behind my back.
- IF I say no to people, THEN they won't like me and they'll think I'm lazy (and I'll get fired).
- IF I mention this problem to my colleague, THEN it won't be my responsibility later when it blows up.
- IF I stop the kids from doing anything risky, THEN they won't get hurt and I won't get blamed for it.
- IF I check the post, THEN I might get a bill for something unexpected and I'll be broke.
- IF people don't act a certain way towards me, THEN they're disrespecting me.
- IF I get certain material things, THEN people will like me and be impressed by me.
- IF I have thoughts of harming somebody, THEN I'm a horrible person.
- IF I don't get rid of these thoughts, THEN I'll never be able to live the life I want.
- IF I do compulsions for an hour, THEN I can do my work without distraction.
- IF everything else around me changed, THEN my life would be better.
- IF I could find the right medication, THEN I wouldn't have these mental health challenges.

IS YOUR WORLD BUILT ON MAGICAL THINKING?

In mental healthcare, the term 'magical thinking' typically refers to something such as a girl believing she can prevent her parents from having a car accident if she prays in a particular way without having any impure thoughts: IF X (I pray correctly and purely) THEN Y (my parents will be safe). This also logically implies that IF X (I pray incorrectly and blasphemously) THEN Y (I'll be responsible for my parents' death). If she enjoys the sense of relief and certainty she gets when she does the prayer 'correctly', she's setting herself up for the inevitable but totally logical anxiety that will result when she does it 'incorrectly'. She's guaranteed to have thoughts she judges as impure, which will lead to repeating the prayers over and over again to get them 'right'.

This is the trap of magical thinking. If you believe the action will prevent what you're afraid of, you're setting up your brain to believe that not performing that action will cause your fears to come true. And then when you don't perform that action, or don't perform it correctly, you panic and anxiety spikes; it's as though not performing that action is equivalent to making your fears come true. And this extends way beyond things people consider 'magical' or 'delusional'.

It's the same pattern at work if you believe you need to change your body to look a particular way before people will love you or value you. This is a belief that supplement manufacturers, gyms, the media, your friends, and your family members may all participate in promoting. But it's delusional. It's a belief that rituals will control the thoughts of others. And it's a trap. If you tell your brain you must look a particular way to be valued, then you logically set yourself up to not feel valued if you don't look that way.

If you believe your partner loves you because he sends you lengthy messages sprinkled with emojis, then it's only natural that you become anxious when he sends you short messages without emojis. If you want that warm, loving feeling you get when you open the loquacious, emoji-filled message, you're also choosing the panicked uncertainty of reading a one-word reply or, heaven forbid, no reply at all ☹.

It's this same pattern at work if you believe you need to drink alcohol or do drugs to be creative. Even if you simply believe you need the right kind of notebook, the right types of pen or a perfectly quiet environment before you do any work, you're walking right into the trap. You'll have to drink more and more, or get higher and higher, or find a quieter and quieter place, until you stop creating completely because your brain won't let you satisfy the first part of the equation.

As we discussed in the previous chapter, if you believe you need to have a specific feeling before you can do what matters to you, trying to chase that feeling consumes you and leaves nothing for what matters. When you cut out compulsions, you break that IF X THEN Y pattern.

SO WHAT'S THE ALTERNATIVE?

Luckily, the alternative is an equation with only one variable: IF X THEN X. That's it. Just X. Accept things for what they are. No judgements or magical thinking or discrimination or over-reaction necessary. The antidote to this pattern of thinking is the practice of mindfulness. As you practise mindfulness and meditation more in your life, you're going to find that it becomes easier to break this pattern and simply be with the experience you're having.

In the past, you might have believed something like: IF X (I feel stressed) THEN Y (I can't be myself around my friends), but now, if you feel stressed, that's great, you feel stressed. It doesn't have any meaning you don't give to it. You can do the things you care about while feeling stressed. This is mindfulness at work. You can have emotions or thoughts. What you choose to do while having those emotions or thoughts is entirely separate.

WHAT ABOUT SELF-ESTEEM?

I'm opposed to self-esteem. Or I should say: I'm opposed to how we generally approach self-esteem, as a self-image propped up by this IF X THEN Y pattern. IF I get compliments, IF I make lots of money, IF I'm desired, IF I gain more followers, IF I get gold stars, IF people say I'm smart, IF I have the best titles, IF I get all the likes, IF I do it right, IF I'm invited to special events, IF I reach the goal, IF I'm better than you, IF I'm not wrong, IF I win ... THEN I'm valuable.

The pursuit of self-esteem logically sets you up for low self-esteem. It's the same trap again: if you believe your value comes from people giving you things, then you hand over control of your self-image to other people. If they don't give you those things, then your brain logically concludes you must not be valuable. In this situation you can begin to see how chasing desirable feelings we think of as 'good' can actually set us up for the feelings we don't like. You will spend much more time not getting compliments than you will spend getting compliments. So if your self-worth depends on compliments, expect your self-worth to be low.

Your value is in your existence. It's innate and unchanging. It does not come from other people. If you hand over control of your value to others, expect them to waste it. They won't know you've put them in charge of the only thing you own. Take back your self. Remove self-esteem from the equation.

You are awesome. Proceed accordingly. The next exercise, the Awesome Schedule, will help you with that. We're doing this exercise here because it's such an effective way to bring healthy activities into your life without relying on that IF X THEN Y pattern. It's all about proactively doing the things you want as part of your life, instead of doing them reactively or waiting to do them until after you've captured some feeling.

EXERCISE: The Awesome Schedule

The Awesome Schedule is all about doing things that help you to be healthy and happy, regardless of how you feel or what's happening in your life. You can always support yourself. It's not something you do after you get a special feeling or reach a particular point in life. You can start doing it right now.

The Awesome Schedule is a simple way of helping you support the practice of being yourself (which is awesome). Here's how:

1. Grab a calendar or open up your digital schedule. Make sure you're doing this exercise in something you already use. If you don't use a calendar to schedule in events, grab some sticky-notes you can place in a visible location. Also grab some paper you can brainstorm on, or use the sticky-notes.
2. Consider your values. Take a look at your Ideal Inventory exercise (page 34). Consider the experiences you've had in life with which you felt especially engaged or happy.
3. What types of activity support any or all of those? What activities help you be healthy and happy? What do you always enjoy doing? What do you wish you did more often? You might want to write your answers down on a piece of paper so you can brainstorm a bit here. Write down whatever comes to mind. Just get it out of your head and on to paper.
4. Of the activities that you wrote down, pick one that you enjoy doing simply for its own sake. Make sure it's something you can do.
5. Commit to doing that once a month. Schedule it in. How will you make that a regular part of your life?
6. Do it.
7. Keep adding to your Awesome Schedule as you show yourself that you can do things you enjoy, not to control your feelings or to get things, but as an expression of who you are.

EVERYTHING YOU WANT TO DO IN LIFE IS ON THE OTHER SIDE OF AN ENORMOUS BATH FULL OF THOUGHTS AND FEELINGS YOU'VE TRIED TO AVOID

STEP 9

Stop checking

The very first exercise we did at the beginning of the book (page 13) – to not check your phone when you get the urge to check it – was an exercise to practise the basics of cutting out checking compulsions. You get an urge, you accept that it's there, and you choose how you want to act. It's an opportunity to break that IF X THEN Y pattern. You can experience an urge to check without reacting to it or trying to make it go away. Checking your phone might be something you consider 'normal', but it's in those normal behaviours that we train our brains to react to uncertainty, anxiety and other feelings we don't like – and I'm telling you that as somebody who was on the extreme end of disordered checking.

Compulsive checking was a major part of my struggle with mental illness. I could spend hours online reloading sites and checking social media accounts for responses to messages or comments. I would set my alarm and then check that I'd set it, and then reset it and check again, and then set two or three more alarms because I wasn't certain I could be sure they were set. I checked every appliance and lock and plug in my home. I was constantly checking I still had everything on me that I needed. I checked how people were looking at me. I checked memories of conversations over and over again to be certain I hadn't said something offensive or done something horrible. I was checking for reassurance, checking receipts, checking for stains, checking my fly was done up, checking how I smelled, and checking and checking ... But it was a practice I trained my brain into, built on a solid foundation of totally normal, socially acceptable checking.

WHERE IS MY WATER BOTTLE?

One night as I was walking home from the gym, I started to wonder if I'd put my water bottle back in my gym bag when I left the locker room. I'd recently forgotten my water bottle there and had bought a new one – the nice shiny yellow one I was now worried I'd forgotten.

So there was an uncertainty. It was something that had happened before. It had cost me money – not much, but money I didn't need to spend. I would feel even worse if I had to spend more money on another water bottle simply because I hadn't paid attention. This isn't delusional. Worrying that I had forgotten my water bottle is a 'legitimate worry', right?

To add some context to this situation: I'd been recovered from mental illness for about six years, and it was around the time I was writing this book. At that time, under no criteria would I have been classified as having any mental illness. I'd say I was physically and mentally in great shape. I was a totally sane, rational human being worried about forgetting something. All I had to do was open my gym bag and check if the bottle was there. I was still close enough to the gym that I could run back and grab it.

Let's pause here. What would you do in this situation? Based on everything you've read so far, what do you think I did?

I didn't check. I kept on walking. When I got home, I put my bag down and still didn't open it. Later, when I wanted a drink, I pulled my water bottle out of my bag.

Checking whether I had my water bottle might not seem like it has anything to do with mental health. But if we look at the pattern of behaviour there, what was happening? I experienced an uncertainty (what if forgot my water bottle?), that triggered emotions I didn't like (fear of wasting money, fear of losing something, fear of being responsible for something going wrong), and then I wanted to do something to get rid of those feelings.

Although it may seem 'normal', checking for a water bottle would be no different than checking with three different doctors to make sure they all agree that your lymph nodes aren't abnormally swollen, or checking and rechecking the email you have just sent your boss to make sure you didn't make any mistakes that might get you fired, or checking the door and window locks multiple times before bed, or constantly seeking reassurance from your partner so you can be certain they still love you.

I didn't check because I didn't want to train my brain to give me more uncertainties and more anxieties to chase after. If I had checked and it was there, I would've been happy. My brain would have registered that and, in the future, it would have given me more uncertainties so I could try to get rid of those and find the same happiness. If I had checked and the bottle wasn't there, I would have been upset and run back to the gym, and my brain would have registered that losing a water bottle is a very bad thing and we should worry about losing things even more in the future so we can avoid being responsible for bad things happening.

Brains are logical and helpful. When it comes to compulsions, even the compulsions that seem most absurdly irrational grow very logically from reasonable, everyday activities. Let's look at an example of a helpful, logical brain doing what it does best.

THE TOTALLY LOGICAL PROGRESSION OF A MENTAL ILLNESS

Assume that I did check my bag. The bottle would have been there and I'd have felt relieved. But then my brain, helpful brain that it is, would want me to again experience that amazing feeling of relief. It might even try to help me get that experience right away by tossing out an uncertainty about my wallet and my keys. I always keep them in my gym bag and since my hand was already in there, I should make sure they hadn't been stolen at the gym. If I'm worried about wasting money on a water bottle, losing my wallet or having somebody steal my keys to break into my apartment and take all of my valuables would be far worse than losing a water bottle, right? It only makes sense.

And if losing valuables is a bad thing, well, there's so many different ways that could happen, so my brain would be on the look-out for other uncertainties that could lead to me losing resources. What if I left the patio door open? What if I didn't lock my gym locker? What if somebody copied my bank card? What if I didn't lock the front door when I left this morning? What if I left the car unlocked? What if the windows are all open? It'd be stupid if I constantly checked for my wallet but I didn't check all of that other stuff. Somebody could walk right into my home or log in to my bank account and take everything I owned. That would be far more devastating than losing my wallet. At least, even if all that did happen, I'd still have my job. I could make money to get my life back. But what if I lost my job? There's so many ways that could happen. What if I say something stupid in a meeting or an email and everybody thinks I'm not a 'good fit'? What if I say the wrong thing to a customer? What if something gets stolen and I get blamed for it? What if they find out I lied a bit (a lot) on my application? What if I miss an important deadline? What if somebody else on my team screws up and people think it's my fault? What if I damage something at work and I have to pay for it? What if I don't set the security alarm properly when I'm leaving? What if my laptop battery catches fire and burns down the entire office? I left it plugged in and charging when I went to a meeting, the meeting went on late so I wasn't going to return to the office and get it, but the adapter gets so hot when the laptop is charging, and laptop batteries do catch fire. So should I go back to the office and get it? I planned to meet friends for dinner but I could tell them I'm working late. They'll understand.

It's one thing to lose something of mine, but if I'm responsible for damaging other people's valuables, then I have to pay for them and I'll feel so guilty. The office building, at least, is empty at night and the company would have insurance, but what if I was responsible for burning down my apartment building? I'd be paying for that for the rest of my life. What if I left the toaster plugged in? Or I left my desktop computer running and it overheated? What if there was some paper or a cloth near something that could get hot? What if I spilt something flammable on the floor and a spark from a plug set it on fire? What if I left the stove on? If I'm going to check to make sure I hadn't lost my water bottle, surely it's reasonable to check that I turned off the stove. There was this old stove in the apartment I was renting and it had knobs that could actually pop off – it had happened to me before when I'd turned them too quickly. Then I couldn't know if it was actually turned to high or low or off or burn-the-building-down. The knobs could also turn in any direction. You could turn it clockwise or anti-clockwise indefinitely. So even if the knob was in the off position, it might only look that way and could actually be slightly to the right, which would put it at the highest setting. If I turned it off quickly, it was easy to pop it right past the off position into the high position. I'd done it before. So it made sense to check the knobs were actually in the off position by wiggling them, then to wait for a bit and touch the hob to make sure it wasn't heating up. Because what if I'd actually turned it on by wiggling the knob to make sure it was off? At least one thing working in my favour was the fact that it was an electric stove, so when it was set to high, the hob would glow red hot. So to really make sure it wasn't on, all I had to do was wait in front of the stove and watch the rings to make sure they didn't turn red. But what if there was some type of malfunction inside? It's plugged into that big outlet in the back. If they couldn't even design the knobs well, is it inconceivable to think that the rest of the stove might be poorly designed? What's stopping something from breaking inside the stove, something I can't see or check, and turning the entire appliance into an apartment fire-starter and burning up all the old ladies and their cats? And it would be ALL MY FAULT.

Shouldn't everybody be standing in front of their stove right now watching it?

That's why I didn't check if my water bottle was in my bag.

TOWARDS PLEASURE, AWAY FROM PAIN, INTO A BOTTOMLESS PIT

When you seek relief from uncertainty, you reinforce two feedback loops in your brain that guarantee more uncertainty.

The first loop is all about positive rewards. Relief from uncertainty will make me feel good! Now my brain needs to find more uncertainties so I can try to get rid of them and get that wonderful feeling I want again. Remember: relief from uncertainty requires uncertainty. You're making uncertainty a prerequisite for feeling good.

It helped me to approach all of my mental health challenges as addictions. As long as I chase that feeling I want, I'm choosing to experience the opposite. The withdrawal is inevitable.

The second loop is all about avoiding danger. When you react to an uncertainty you're sending a loud message to your brain: 'If this thing I'm worried about actually happened, it would be terrible! It's dangerous. I have to avoid it.' Your brain likes to protect you from danger so it's going to helpfully look for all of the ways that dangerous thing might happen. If you worry about a friend posting embarrassing photos of you online after a night out, so you keep checking to see if they've posted anything, that tells your brain you're worried about what people will think about you. So your brain will start to look for other ways that you might get embarrassed: What if you stink? What if somebody accuses you of a crime you didn't commit? What if somebody is recording you naked in the bathroom and they're going to share the video online? And then you'll have to start checking to make sure all of those aren't coming true.

When these two loops get spinning together, it's disastrous. But it doesn't happen instantly. Checking my water bottle that night wouldn't have sent me immediately spiralling down into a compulsive pit of despair. Getting these loops going takes practice, just as stopping them will take time and practice.

BUT WHAT IF MY COMPULSIONS DON'T BOTHER ME?

Most won't. It's entirely possible they won't seem to interfere with your life. That doesn't mean they're not part of the problem. You might notice that checking on your kids constantly is affecting your life – and theirs – negatively, but all of the checking you do at work or in your relationship with your partner might seem useful. But all compulsions are practices. Do you want to be skilled at them? Do you want to keep getting better at them until you notice that they're causing you distress?

We currently have this illness-first mental healthcare system that's focused on symptoms and crises. You have to get sick to get help. We pretend that people who aren't in crisis don't have problematic mental health and don't need to take care of it. This is built into the systems governing how we approach mental healthcare. In the *Diagnostic and Statistical Manual of Mental Disorders 5*, the hefty tome published by the American Psychiatric Association providing criteria to diagnose mental illnesses, there's a clause in the diagnostic criteria for OCD that I call the 'distress clause'. You can find this in the criteria for other disorders as well, such as bipolar disorder (twice), social anxiety disorder and generalised anxiety disorder. There are variations in other disorders as well. The distress clause for OCD says that obsessions/compulsions must be time-consuming, or 'cause clinically significant distress or impairment in social, occupational, or other important areas of functioning'.[14]

Imagine if we did this in other areas of healthcare, such as heart disease. Your doctor would see that your blood pressure is getting high and your cholesterol is in the danger zone, but you're not distressed by it, so what's the problem? It's not impairing your functioning. You like sitting all day! Keep eating the way you're eating. You love cheeseburgers! Keep not exercising the way you're not exercising. Drink all night! Come back when you're lying on the floor clutching your chest and then we can discuss healthier behaviours because you've become distressed and your functioning is presumably now impaired sufficiently to classify as 'clinically significant'.

You don't need to wait for a heart attack. You don't need to wait for a mental illness. Simply on practical terms, if you spend less time and energy reacting to uncertainty, you'll have more time to put into building and creating things you actually care about. Let your values guide you here. Something doesn't need to be 'bad' or an 'illness' to be something you kick out of your life. Is it helping you to be happy and healthy over the long term?

THE PRACTICE OF ELIMINATING A CHECKING COMPULSION

Some uncertainties are scarier than others. 'What if I received an email?' might not trigger as much anxiety in you as: 'What if my phone overheats while charging beside my bed and it causes a fire that kills me?'

I find that the ACT model of accepting the stuff in your head, choosing a direction aligned with your values, and then taking action is especially useful for dealing with uncertainties about frightening possibilities because, by taking action while accepting that those fears are there, you show your brain that it doesn't need to be afraid. Similar to the coping compulsions example in Step 7, I'll go through this using that ACT structure again, and I'll add two tricks that can help with overcoming terrifying uncertainties. We'll explore this using a common fear: that I might have left the stove on, it'll cause lots of damage, it might kill somebody, and I'll be blamed for it. Before we get into that, there are two things I want to explain:

1. Dealing with a compulsion like checking the stove is probably one you'll do further up your Hierarchy list on page 84. Be honest with yourself about how difficult this might be. Build up your skills by tackling easier compulsions first. It took me significant work to cut out this compulsion.
2. I'm a fan of what's known as *in vivo* exposure. This involves living your life as you want to, which subsequently creates

the opportunities for you to practise cutting out compulsions. To help with that, use the stove as you would like to use it. Don't avoid using the stove so you can reassure yourself you don't need to check it. Of course, if you shrink your life you'll have no anxieties to worry about. Don't do that. In the past, I avoided using the stove to make breakfast so that I wouldn't need to check it when I left in the morning. That's a compulsion. I love breakfasts. There's so many wonderful breakfasts I can make myself if I use the stove. So I started using the stove for breakfast every day. That created the uncertainty I could practise accepting without trying to use checking compulsions to get rid of it.

Now let's dive into the practice of cutting out this compulsion:

I accept the stuff in my head and practise being present

- After using the stove for breakfast, I would get ready to leave. Inevitably, at that point my brain would start to worry about whether I had turned off the stove or not. Not checking the stove would create an incredible amount of anxiety. I would physically feel terrible. I'd be irritable. I'd be on the verge of a panic attack. I would hear people shouting at me for burning down the building. And I can accept all of that. It's OK for that uncertainty and subsequent anxiety to be there. That's an experience I can have in the present.
- When cutting out compulsions that cause significant anxiety, there are two different approaches that have helped me. In a little ebook called *The Acceptance Field Guide* that I wrote early in my peer-support career, I called these The Two Tricks. They might seem contradictory. Test them out. You may find they work in different situations, on different days. Sometimes I would sit with the question about whether the stove was on. At other times, I would accept the consequences. Both were useful to practise. Here's how they work:

Trick No.1: Sit with the question

Why do we answer the questions our brains throw at us? It was an incredible revelation the day I realised I didn't have to answer them. Why had nobody ever told me that?! It took about 29 years to learn that I don't actually have to be certain about the uncertainties in my head. If my brain throws a ball, I don't have to chase it. I'm not a dog. If my brain is wondering if the stove is on, it can wonder that. Maybe it is on. Maybe it isn't. I don't have to answer. My brain doesn't know if the stove is on or if I turned it off! That uncertainty can be there. I can feel uncertain and carry it with me, unresolved, as I do the things I value.

Trick No.2: Accept the consequences

This is basically the complete opposite of the first trick. It's by far my favourite recovery skill but it's not for beginners. It's possible I'll never be able to get house insurance after I share this with you but, here we go: using the same powerful imagination I tried using to picture the stove being off, I would instead picture the stove covered in bottles of cleaning supplies and cooking oils, the dishcloths piled on top of them, a greasy frying pan on the hob and all of the rings bright red hot. I'd picture flames licking up around the stove, setting light to the cupboards, the cleaning fluid bottles, the campfire propane canisters that somehow got piled on to the counter beside the stove, and it all exploding in a massive fireball shooting out of the apartment windows. Trying to figure out if I had left the stove on was irrelevant, because I was already responsible for setting the building on fire. It happened. I did it. And I would picture myself coming back to the apartment later, to a crowd of crying people yelling at me as the police handcuffed me and took me away to prison. They'd blame me for setting the fire on purpose. My

picture would be on the news all night. ARSON MURDERER APPREHENDED. I'd be imprisoned for years. My life would be ruined. Nobody would ever want to be near me. I'd be alone and hated for the rest of my life.
- So I would apply one of those tricks, which would bring up even more thoughts and unpleasant emotions, and I can have all of those experiences.

I choose a direction aligned with my values

- After applying one of those tricks, I'm either sitting in a massive amount of uncertainty or I'm convinced my life is over and this is my last day of freedom. My values help pull me through that. If I've used the second trick and I believe I'm going to prison later for burning down my building, I can look to my values to understand how I want to spend my remaining hours of freedom in a way that's healthy, in a way I can be happy about. I can't change the past and what I've done, but I can make sure my next steps are aligned with my values.

I take action

- I don't value engaging in compulsions and making my health worse. So I won't invent a reason to go back into the kitchen so I can covertly check the stove. I'm not going to engage in mental compulsions to try to remember that I turned off the stove so I can reassure myself. I do value going to work to do things that I care about and to see people that I care about. I value contributing to my community. I value taking care of my health.
- So whatever it was that I was leaving my home to go and do, I'm going to leave and do that. I'll intentionally invest my time and energy in what I value.
- Throughout the day, when my brain worries about what I've done, I can repeat these steps all over again and bring my focus back to the valued actions that I'm practising.

TRUSTING YOUR MINDFULNESS PRACTICE

For me, in the past, safety meant worrying about something and then checking it. Worry was the prerequisite for safety.

I was so accustomed to practising mindlessness that my mind was always in a different place when I was cooking, or ironing, or speaking, or driving, so it was totally natural that I'd be anxious about those things. I knew I hadn't paid attention. I didn't know what I'd done. I relied on anxiety to keep me safe. I would often discover that the door was unlocked, the stove was on, that I'd made embarrassing mistakes in emails, I'd miscounted money, I'd almost cut myself with a knife, people noticed I was obviously not paying attention in a conversation. My avid devotion to mindlessness made checking a necessity for survival.

When you remove checking compulsions, you have to do things the first time. You have to be present. You choose not to rely on anxiety anymore.

The practice of mindfulness will be a support for cutting out checking compulsions. You may have noticed that I didn't mention mindfulness in the previous section. That's because I think you'll find the most benefit when you practise mindfulness *before* you feel the urge to compulsively check. Practising mindlessness cultivates the uncertainties that push you into checking.

Even when we practise mindfulness, it's not so that we remember turning off the stove and can reassure ourselves that we did it. It certainly hasn't improved my memory. But I practise mindfulness and I trust in my practice. I trust that when I was at the stove, I was at the stove. I was there cooking. I was there cleaning up. I don't have to remember it. I practise trusting myself, and I show my brain that I trust myself.

When you're practising the checking challenges for this step's exercise, consider how you can deepen your mindfulness practice as a proactive support for handling uncertainty. When checking is no longer an option, what needs to change in your life?

EXERCISE: Checking Challenges

The challenges I explain below are here to give you some extra practice to develop the skills to cut out the checking compulsions you've identified in your Hierarchy.

- **Send an email without rereading it**
  This is so much fun and oh-so-helpful with learning to not lose hours in an email black hole: write an email, don't reread it and send it.

  Be mindful when writing because you won't be coming back to reread those sentences. One way to help yourself with this is to consider how your values translate into writing an email. Before starting to write, pick two or three things you want to give to the recipient. Write words that are aligned with what you want to give. And hit send before your brain knows what's happening! Accept whatever uncertainties pop into your head.

- **Don't check if people are looking at you**
  I always wanted to check if people were looking at me. Then I'd judge what I thought they were thinking about me. As soon as there were people around me, it was as if I wasn't in control of where I looked – I had to make eye contact with everybody. Mostly I wanted to do that because then I would tell myself that people were attracted to me (so I wasn't going to be alone for ever). Thinking about what other people were thinking about me was a compulsion that consumed tremendous amounts of my time.

  Even if you don't experience that compulsion in the same way I did, there might be something else you feel the urge to look at frequently. Practise feeling that urge but not looking, not checking whatever it is that you look at to relieve your uncertainty. Maybe it's checking social

media accounts, checking the news, checking for damage to your vehicle, checking your bank account or checking statistics. Accept that the urge is there. Accept whatever your brain throws at you. Maybe the most attractive person ever is looking at you and because you didn't return their smouldering gaze, you'll never hook up with them and never sail off into the sunset together, and you'll end up alone in a dingy nursing home playing dominos by yourself in a corner.

- **Don't check your reflection**
  Try not checking how you look when you feel the urge. Maybe there is something in your teeth. Maybe your hair is all wrong. Maybe there are stains down the front of your trousers. Practise accepting whatever uncertainties arise when you don't react to those urges to check. What do they tell you about your fears? Try practising the Two Tricks we looked at earlier. Sometimes you'll find it useful to sit with the uncertainty and not check. At other times, practise accepting the extreme consequences of your worries.

DON'T MAKE ILLNESS THE PREREQUISITE FOR HEALTH

STEP 10

Understand your fears

> 'In terms of what's helped me the most in recovery is understanding that all my mental health issues were interrelated. Although on the surface they appeared as different themes, at its roots I could break them down to a couple of ideas. It was also very useful for me to understand that I have control over the things that I want to do!'
>
> Denis

As you're clearing away these compulsions, you'll start to see an ugly monster or two chewing away at you underneath them, as we talked about way back in Step 2: 'Recognise your problems'. The massive range of specific symptoms we think we're struggling with are the superficial expressions of only a few underlying fears. Trying to deal with each symptom as a separate issue is like clearing out a massive warehouse full of a million individual pieces of rubbish. With each piece you pick up, you uncover another one underneath. There's always another anxiety, always another urge, always another compulsion to replace the one you've cleared away. But when you recognise these as patterns and you see the commonalities that link all of these challenges together, it's as though the rubbish is already collected together in a couple of enormous bags. You can take a big marker and write your fear on each bag. Here is all the junk I collected in reaction to my fear of death. Here is a bag full of the hearts I smashed up avoiding my fear of being alone. Here is a bag full of everything I hoarded because I was afraid I wouldn't have enough.

WHAT IF I GET POISONED?

One of the fears I struggled with was that somebody would try to poison me. At the gym, in particular, I wouldn't leave my water bottle unattended. If I forgot it somewhere, or even let it out of my sight temporarily, I'd get very anxious. When I found it again I wouldn't drink out of it. I'd check to see if it looked like it had been tampered with, I'd empty it, rinse it out, dry it with paper towels and, even then, I can remember times when I wouldn't use it again until I could wash it a few times.

Superficially, this was a paranoid fear that somebody was trying to hurt me. But underneath that was a fear of death. My brain was very imaginative when it came to thinking of ways I could die. I had many compulsions connected to the fear of death.

The traditional way of help through Cognitive Behavioural Therapy (CBT) would have focused on trying to help me see how unlikely or irrational it was to believe that somebody was trying to poison me. It would have been about labelling that thought as a 'cognitive distortion' or a paranoid thought and then adding up evidence to see why it was unlikely. But I never found that approach helpful. I could always think of a reason why, as unlikely as it might be, the fear was possible. My brain was as skilled at debating as it was at inventing creative ways to die. And debating about whether a thought is irrational or rational misses the underlying fear: death. It doesn't matter what label we stick on the thought, it's simply a sign pointing to the real issue.

Getting over my compulsions around being poisoned was about

accepting the superficial fear (somebody will poison or infect my water bottle) and then also accepting the consequences of that (dying), which is what I was actually afraid of. This is where that second trick of accepting consequences, which I explained in the previous step (page 111), comes in handy.

I would pick up the water bottle, recognise that my brain was throwing out all these thoughts about the bottle being poisoned or infected, and I'd take a drink from it. I wouldn't engage in any compulsions. My brain would freak out because I was now going to die. I would agree with it. I was about to die, painfully, missing out on everything I'd ever wanted to do in life, choking out my last breath all alone later that night on the floor of my apartment in a pile of regrets and vomit. However, since this would be my last workout, I would enjoy it. I would appreciate everything my body does for me. I wouldn't check how I looked in the mirror or avoid any exercises because I was afraid of failing, getting injured or looking stupid. I would stick to my values and give myself a great workout, enjoying my last few moments of being able to use my body.

This is tough. It will make you sweat. Cutting out compulsions might seem very difficult because all of the fears or uncertainties you're reacting to are terrifying. They are the complete opposite of what you want in life. You don't want to lose your job, or have your relationship end, or see anything bad happen to your children, or lose all of your money or be hated by everybody – I understand that. I know exactly how it feels to believe that you've just harmed somebody or that you're about to die or that you've done any number of horrible things your brain can imagine, and believe them completely, without a shred of doubt. There is, however, incredible power in showing your brain it doesn't need to be afraid of those experiences any longer. You can show your brain that those experiences, ones that you've invested so many hours and days in trying to prevent, can happen. And not only can they happen, they've already happened. They're in the past now. You're not a time traveller so you can't change the past. All you can do is be in the present.

You can be yourself now. You can act according to your values. You can trust yourself to handle this.

YOUR BRAIN IS TRYING TO HELP YOU

Our brains are trying to help us prevent the experiences we want to avoid. If you're afraid of death, your brain will start looking for all the different ways you could die. As you react to more and more of the ways your brain thinks you could die, it helpfully finds even more uncertainties about death for you to control. This very natural progression expands through your life until you're constantly obsessing and spending all your time and energy trying to prevent your death. It's an unfortunate way to miss out on living.

I don't want to make a sweeping generalisation but ... we're all going to die. You'll die. I'll die. Everybody you know will die. Everybody you don't know will die. This is a reality of life. Like jumping in a pool and getting wet; when we jump into life, we surely experience death.

The previous steps might have sparked some thoughts about death. What if I don't check the door lock and somebody breaks in and kills me? What if I'm responsible for an accident that kills other people? What if this feeling in my chest is actually a heart attack and the doctor is wrong that I'm only having a panic attack?!

When you're able to recognise what you're afraid of at a deeper level, you can be kind and understanding to your brain when it throws up another uncertainty. Your brain is trying to protect you. It's like a little child that doesn't want anything bad to happen to you. It can't understand why you're not doing compulsions anymore. If you've taught your brain to be very afraid of death, it's only natural that it's constantly worrying about things that might cause you to die.

Although it's important to cut out compulsions, until you learn how to practise accepting the fears at the roots of your compulsions, your brain will always find something new to latch on to. If you stop researching illness symptoms online, your brain might move on to obsessing about toxins in your food, or finding the 'right' vitamins. If you stop trying to reassure yourself that you're not a murderer, your brain might move on to obsessing about your sexuality, or whether you're a rapist, or something else that you feel is the exact opposite of who you are. If you stop trying to control your co-workers, you may notice yourself trying to control your girlfriend.

Use this next exercise to dig deep underneath your compulsions. Find those big uncertainties you're trying to avoid. You can use the skills we're exploring to accept those uncertainties and get comfortable with them. When you can do that, your brain can stop worrying about them.

EXERCISE: **The Five Whys**

When we dig into the fears that bother us, commonalities beneath seemingly disparate fears and uncertainties begin to emerge. The Five Whys is an exercise from the world of design and business that can help you dig under your fears and find those common roots. It can help you see why you're doing what you're doing. Here's how to do the exercise:

1. Pick one of your compulsions.
2. Ask yourself: 'Why would it be bad to stop doing that?'
3. Then take your answer and ask yourself: 'Why would *that* be bad (or wrong, or unwanted, etc.)?'
4. Answer that question, and again ask yourself why that would be bad.
5. Repeat this question-and-answer process a total of five times and see where you land.

Here's an example of how this works:

Compulsion: Rereading messages from your partner or somebody you're dating

Q1) Why would it be bad to stop rereading those messages?
A1) Because then I couldn't be certain about what they truly mean.
Q2) Why would it be bad not to know what the messages truly mean?
A2) Because I have to know if that person is still interested in me or not.
Q3) Why would it be bad if you didn't know whether they were still interested in you?
A3) Because I'm not going to waste my time investing in a relationship if they're not interested in me.
Q4) Why wouldn't you want to invest in a relationship if it won't be reciprocated?
A4) Because I could be putting that into a relationship with the right person who I am going to spend the rest of my life with.
Q5) Why would it be bad to put everything into a relationship with the wrong person?
A5) Because I would feel so ripped off. I'd end up giving everything and then I'd be left there all alone while the person I should've been with will have gone off to be with somebody else.

Notice how we went from checking and rereading messages to something that's much more fundamental about how that person approaches relationships. His actions are all about avoiding things he's afraid of (being with the wrong person, losing the investment of his resources, being alone) instead of trying to create something he actually wants to experience. If he looked at other areas of his life, he'd probably see that he's taking a similarly transactional and fear-based approach in business relationships and friendships – always holding back, averse to risk, letting fear guide his actions, waiting for the other person to commit fully and give more. Although the compulsions around rereading messages might bother him the most, if he doesn't want these fears to continually pop up in the form of new compulsions, he can help himself by accepting more uncertainty and taking a more proactive, value-based approach in all of his relationships.

*

As you do this exercise, modify the questions to fit the context, and push into difficult subjects. You may need to ask more than five questions. And keep an open mind. Many of the ways you see yourself reacting to those root fears or uncertainties in your everyday actions may not be things you've defined as compulsions. They may be ways of thinking and behaving you feel are part of your personality. However, consider that they may all be ways you cultivate and maintain that fear.

WHY DO YOU DO WHAT YOU DO?

STEP 11

Stop controlling

In *The Trial*, by Franz Kafka, there's a parable that a priest tells the main character, K., as a way of explaining a common delusion people possess about the Law. The parable goes something like this: a man, arriving at an open door – the entrance to the Law – is greeted by a frightening-looking guard standing beside the doorway. The man requests admittance to the Law but the guard tells him that he can't go through the door just yet, and if he tries to go through, the guard can't be responsible for the terrible things that might happen to the man. There are even more frightening guards ahead. The door is ajar but the man is not sure what's on the other side. He decides not to risk it. He'll wait until it's the right time to enter. So he waits. Sometimes the guard chats with him. The man gives up all his possessions to bribe the guard for admittance to the Law, but to no avail. The man grows very old waiting. Year after year, he sits by the door, hoping the right time to enter will soon arrive. And then, one day, the man, by now very old and feeling that he's on the verge of death, notices a light flooding out from the doorway. He looks up at the guard. Surely this is a sign that the right time has finally come. He asks the guard if it's time. In answer to the man's last question, the guard explains that this particular door was meant only for that man and now that he's dying, the guard will shut the door. The man dies.[15]

Best. Story. Ever.

What that man did at the door is a typical controlling compulsion: avoidance. He was uncertain about something bad happening and he tried to control that uncertainty by not taking the actions he actually wanted to take in life. He might have felt that he was avoiding suffering, but the result was a lifetime of suffering and he didn't go where he wanted to go.

THE NATURE OF CONTROLLING BEHAVIOURS

Controlling compulsions are the actions we take to control everybody around us, the future, the past, and everything imaginable in the universe to avoid uncertainty, anxiety and other feelings we don't like. For example:

- A young man who restricts his food intake and exercises obsessively because he thinks the image he sees in the mirror looks wrong and he wants to 'correct' it.
- The woman who lies about her age and posts flattering pictures from several years ago on her dating profile because she's afraid of not getting any messages.
- A manager who creates systems in her office that depend on every decision going through her so she can be certain nobody makes a mistake that will affect her performance review.
- When a boy turns his video game console off and on in a precise order and needs to play segments of a new game 'cleanly', without any mistakes, to prevent his personality being stolen.
- A woman who tries to control what her girlfriend does and where she goes because she's afraid she'll meet somebody better and leave her.

Of course, that young man will only see more and more things wrong in the mirror. That woman will experience even worse rejection when her dates discover she isn't the person she presented herself to be on her profile. That manager's projects will fail because of the oversight bottlenecks she creates from fear of failure. That boy will need to play the game over and over again and he'll get so agitated about it that his parents will wonder what happened to their son. And that woman will scare her girlfriend away.

The more you control, the more you must control. That is the nature of controlling. Only commit to it if you want more of the uncertainties you're trying to control.

But how do you stop trying to control the universe and everybody in it? Especially when we're only trying to control the universe to prevent terrible things from happening, like death.

THE PRACTICE OF ELIMINATING A CONTROLLING COMPULSION

Notice in this example, as well, how checking compulsions are tightly wound up with controlling compulsions. You'll often find that you experience uncertainty, you check, you judge what you check, which creates more uncertainty, and then you try to control that uncertainty.

We'll go through this example using the same ACT format as the previous examples: accepting and being present with whatever is happening in your head; choosing a direction that you value; and then acting in a way that's aligned with your values.

In this example, I'll share how I practised overcoming that fear that I was going to be poisoned.

I accept the stuff in my head and practise being present

- I would purposefully trigger the stuff in my head by leaving my water bottle unattended while I went to get a towel from another part of the gym.
- When I'd return to pick up my bottle, my brain would start throwing up all these thoughts about whether somebody might have touched the bottle or poisoned it. I was also anxious about contracting diseases so the worries in my brain were always

a mix of poisoning and whatever disease I was afraid of that week. I often referred to it as 'HIVebolaherpes'. It's totally fine that I have those thoughts and feel anxious. I know my brain is reacting to my fear of death.

- I would agree with all of the thoughts that came up. I would use that second trick of accepting the consequences: I would be poisoned the moment I took a drink out of my bottle. I would die later that day, slowly and painfully. Even if the poison didn't kill me, somebody had probably rubbed infected blood around the rim of the bottle and, because I often bit the inside of my cheek while I had anxious dreams at night, the disease would get into my bloodstream. People would doubt my story about how I got the disease. Nobody would ever want to date me. I wouldn't get to accomplish any of the things I'd wanted to do in life.

I choose a direction aligned with my values

- I'd feel an intense urge to check if there was anything like blood on the bottle or anywhere around it. I would also feel the urge to check the people nearby to see if anybody looked suspicious. But I'm focused on actions, not obsessions, so I'm not going to engage in compulsions as a reaction to the obsessions. I'll choose to do something aligned with my values. I'm at the gym, so how can I support my exercise practice? Since I'm about to die, how do I want to spend my last hours or my last day? I would consider what I could do that's aligned with who I am and what I care about. Spending my last day reacting to the stuff in my head is not something I value.

I take action

- It's important to be hydrated when working out, so I would unscrew the cap, take a drink, making sure to touch my lips to the rim (that was something I often avoided doing in the past),

and then I'd swallow and go straight to the next exercise without looking at the water bottle.
- I would keep working out as intensely as I was before I poisoned myself. This is so important because it shows my brain that I'm not afraid. I'm indicating to my brain that it was wrong to bring up this anxiety. The labels I've attached to death and disease were incorrect. I don't have to react to death or disease with panic and avoidance. I can welcome them and do what I care about. If it's my last workout, I'd better have a great session. There's no point in saving some energy for tomorrow or not doing squats because I'm afraid of hurting my knees. I can practise mindfulness and enjoy the movement of my body, the racing of my heart, a deep exhale as I push the weights, the sunlight shining through the windows, the music, all of the people around me sweating away, each with their own anxieties, their own suffering, their own hopes for themselves and their families.

COMPLEX CONTROLLING COMPULSIONS

While accepting that I might get killed seems intense, it's relatively simple — I accept that I will die and I do what I value. There are many instances where eliminating a controlling compulsion is emotionally intense but quite straightforward — you accept that you'll die, be hated, cause an accident, get fired, be dumped, etc., and you do what you value. In many situations, however, for instance at work, in relationships, in society or politics, controlling is all we've ever known. We still want to reach our goals at work, we still want to have relationships, so how do we do that without controlling?

Part Two of this book is all about making that shift away from your control addiction towards a life of accepting uncertainty and doing what you value. We'll explore many ways of doing that. So for this exercise, you'll practise flexing your imagination in a way that can help you open up alternatives to the catastrophising that fuels our need to control everything.

EXERCISE: **Practising Possibility**

For years, in any situation, my mind would do something I called 'going from A to Z to the end of the world'. When presented with nearly any situation, real or imagined, I would immediately experience the worst possible outcome. I mentioned some examples of this in the Introduction, such as when I would walk up steps, and see myself falling and feel my teeth get smashed in. Those types of experience happened constantly. If I was walking across a drain cover in the road, I'd see it collapsing and me getting stuck in a muddy hole, so I'd walk around it. If I thought about cooking a dish to take to a friend's dinner party, my mind would quickly imagine me chopping off my fingers while preparing the vegetables, so I would convince myself I should buy something instead and say I was too busy to cook. At the gym, when I thought about picking up some free weights, I'd hear somebody angrily yelling at me to put them back because they were using them, so I'd find an empty machine to use instead.

My brain did not know how to imagine anything else happening except the worst possible scenario. So I needed to give my brain the ability to imagine things going well. Like any mental ability, I needed to build that through practice. I needed to practise imagining myself handling challenges. At the same time, I also need to help my brain with cognitive defusion – recognising that all this stuff in my head was nothing more than stuff in my head. And I needed to approach this with the same dedication and passion I had devoted to years of obsessing about the end of the world. Here's how you do it:

1. **Live your life.** Do things you value. While you're doing that, your brain – being the helpful brain that it is – will throw up intrusive thoughts or images about terrible

things happening that will interfere with what you want in life.

2. **When your brain throws up those intrusive thoughts or images, recognise that's just stuff in your head you experience.** It's not you. This can be tricky at first because, in the past (possibly even now) you might have liked that you could always think of the things that could go wrong in any situation. You were the one who spotted the problems in the plans of others. You were the one who took care of your careless family.

3. **Imagine yourself overcoming challenges in the most amazingly fantastical ways.** I'll give you some examples of what I mean. If you often worry about accidents when you're driving, the next time you notice your brain starting to worry about you getting hit, you could picture yourself masterfully manoeuvring around the potential danger like you're a trained stunt-car driver in a movie, swerving and dodging and speeding out of danger.

   If you're going on holiday to a remote island and you're worried about getting sick or hurt, you might instead imagine yourself riding a dolphin to the island just in time to attend a parade in your honour with all the most delicious foods you could ever eat. If you're worried about having a panic attack on the flight there, you might picture yourself leading everybody in the aircraft in a choreographed dance number, with the flight attendants doing cartwheels out on the wings while miniature unicorns prance up and down the aisles.

   If you worry about loved ones getting hurt, your brain probably discovers many different ways to worry about that. With anything it comes up with, you can try imagining your loved one doing something truly astounding to overcome that challenge. You could picture your spouse dodging an attack and then crushing the attackers with mixed martial arts skills you didn't even know they possessed. You could see your kids flying out of harm's way and carrying all their friends to safety with them. You could image a car swerving into your mother as she slowly crosses the street, but instead of getting hurt by the car, on contact, the vehicle shreds into a million pieces of paper that flutter away in the breeze.

That's all there is to Practising Possibility. You're intentionally imagining things working out fantastically well. It's simple but it might be completely novel for you. You're probably incredibly skilled at imagining horrible things happening. This is a simple practice to build the ability to imagine wonderful things happening. There's nothing wrong with imagining horrible things happening. Practising Possibility is about developing capacity. You're making it possible for your brain to imagine things you couldn't before because you never practised imagining them. When you can imagine wonderful things happening as easily as you can imagine horrible things happening, you give your brain options.

I want to emphasise the importance of adding that fantastical element. This is all stuff in our heads. When you imagine something horrible happening, you probably believe it. The thought doesn't seem separate from reality. This exercise of Practising Possibility helps you show yourself that a totally positive fantasy can as easily exist in your head as a thoroughly negative fantasy. I can imagine myself getting hit by a car as easily as I can imagine myself doing a backflip over a car. They're all thoughts. They're real thoughts. They're not reality.

Doesn't this contradict the trick of accepting consequences?

You could say that. But it's like saying that pull-ups contradict push-ups. You're exercising different muscles. Both are useful. It's like we have different mind muscles. Exercise them all and you'll be capable of adapting to a variety of challenges.

I found that trick of accepting consequences and this exercise of Practising Possibility were particularly helpful with fears I had related to knives. I had to get over the fear of slicing off my fingers and the fear of hurting others. So if I worried about accidentally stabbing somebody, I would picture myself juggling butcher's knives in the air and tossing them around people, or doing summersaults over the kitchen table and catching knives in my teeth. If I was worried about slicing my fingers off, I might just agree with that and see myself without fingers and picture the consequences of that. It's all about going back to that fundamental emotional fitness exercise, finding what's difficult for my brain and then pushing into it so I remove the barriers that get in the way of being myself.

MAKE PEACE WITH DEATH

STEP 12

Tame the monster

As you cut out all of those compulsions and dig down into your fears, you'll uncover this monster that's made up of all your uncertainties, anxieties, urges and other experiences you don't like. For some, the monster is tiny. For others, it's enormous. But we all have this monster and the more we feed it compulsions, the bigger it gets. If you keep feeding it, some parts of your life become off-limits. The monster can get so big that it squeezes you out of your favourite places and activities. It can do nasty things in our lives and leave its stench lingering in our memories.

It's especially difficult to care for a monster like this when you're at work. You might have tried to hide your monster. Maybe you shoved it under your desk so you could keep feeding it and hope nobody noticed. But that only allowed the monster to grow. It became more and more difficult to pretend that there wasn't a monster following you around to project meetings, shredding your work and stinking out the office.

Now that anxious, uncertain, fearful urge monster will try to scare you back into the way you did things before. It will threaten to mess up your relationships, ruin your family holidays, and get you fired from your job. But you don't have to get rid of it. Fighting it will only make it hungrier and angrier and it'll eat you. You can learn how to tame it.

EXPECT THE MONSTER TO PLAY TRICKS ON YOU

When you eliminate compulsions from your life, it's not uncommon to experience physical discomfort, such as headaches, exhaustion, indigestion, ringing in your ears, and whatever else that monster can throw at you to get you anxiously back into compulsions.

In the moments when I would feel an urge to engage in a compulsion and I would choose not to do it, it literally felt as though my brain was shrivelling up inside my head. It was a tingly, painful sensation, like slowly pulling sticking plasters off the inside of my skull.

When I was cutting out online compulsions, choosing to not engage in them would make me fall asleep. I can remember when I was practising not using my computer: I would turn it off, pick up a brand new book I'd purchased specifically for this week of cutting out online compulsions, and the next thing I knew, I'd be waking up at 4 a.m. with all the lights on, having passed out on the sofa early in the evening the moment I tried to read. That went on for about a week until the urge to engage in the compulsion subsided. Change was physically difficult for my brain and I had to make space in my life for that. Weird things will happen.

The monster will come up with reasons why these uncertainties and feelings you're experiencing are different, why you can actually get hurt this time, why you can finally solve this once and for all and it'll never come back if you just do this one compulsion!

Whatever tricks the monster tries to play on you, apply the skills we've been exploring. You can be mindful of the experience and welcome it with curiosity. You don't have to judge it. Don't get caught up in trying to escape the superficial symptoms – it's still the same monster. You don't have to let it push you back into old compulsions, or new ones that feel necessary and 'normal'. You can stick to your values as you ride up and over that Unhappiness Curve (see page 66). As you do that and you act as yourself, you'll grow bigger than the monster and it'll become easier to wrap your arms around it and give it a hug.

YOU ARE NOT YOUR MONSTER (OR YOUR FARTS)

One challenge to taming the monster is that we conflate our identities with our monsters. It's something we learn to do. It's even built into our language. In English, we say things like: 'I'm anxious', or 'I need a shot of whisky', or 'I'm afraid'. We don't see anxiety, or craving, or fear as things we experience or as the by-products of organs. Anxiety is nothing more than brain indigestion but you would never say, 'I'm indigestion'. It's something you experience. You are not your farts. But for some reason, we often believe we are our thoughts, urges, fears and anxieties. Conflating your self with the stuff in your head is what's known as cognitive fusion.

Cognitive *de*fusion is an Acceptance and Commitment Therapy skill that's about recognising that the stuff in your head is stuff you experience. It's not you. Developing your cognitive defusion skills will help create space between you and the stuff in your head. With practice, you can learn to experience whatever the monster spits out and give yourself the space to make a choice about what you want to do with that stuff, if you want to do anything at all.

Regular mindfulness and meditation practice will help you to recognise that you experience thoughts, feelings, or sensations. The previous exercise we looked at, Practising Possibility, is also great for working on cognitive defusion. You get to show your brain how disconnected your thoughts are from reality. The exercise at the end of this step is a variation of a popular ACT exercise that will also help with this skill.

In the past, you might have experienced a fear charging into your mind and knocking you backwards, or an urge that would yank you forward, flat on your face. By developing your cognitive defusion skills, you can recognise that you've run into an urge or a fear. You can see them for what they are; you can steady yourself and not get knocked over by them. Then, recognising that they're not you – they're experiences – you can make a choice about the next step that's actually aligned with your values. You can experience that fear, accept that it's a real fear, but take a step towards it. Or you might notice an urge, accept that it's there, and decide that it is something you want to do, but in an hour or so.

The monster's attempts to push us back into compulsions become experiences that we sense as we take our journey through life. When we no longer conflate those with our selves, they're no longer threatening. We see that the monster can't hurt us. In fact, we can sit right on top of the monster and make it carry us around. The uncertainties and anxieties and other feelings we don't like that the monster spits out become part of the scenery, like clouds floating in the sky.

THOUGHTS ARE LIKE CLOUDS

Cognitive fusion isn't only focused on ourselves. We fuse the stuff in our heads with other people, practices and objects. We say things like: that's disgusting, those people are dangerous, he's wrong, she's a slut and so on. This practice is core to racism, sexism, bigotry and violence. It's very hurtful to ourselves and others. You're using that same skill when you label a thought as something you need to solve, or you judge an experience as something you need to be certain about. You then become very focused on spending all your time and energy on getting rid of those experiences you don't like.

One of the most common questions that comes up in the Everybody has a Brain community online is about how to stop reacting to thoughts, images and memories that people don't like. When people are struggling to stop thinking about something, or stop having some type of reaction, they're struggling with cognitive fusion. Thoughts, urges, images or feelings keep popping up in their heads and they want to do something about them because they're afraid they'll ruin a special event coming up, or they're worried it means they're a monstrous person or they're taking time away from the studying they need to do to graduate. When they have these experiences, they immediately and consistently give those experiences their attention and energy.

When this issue comes up, the question I often suggest that

people consider is this: Why don't you spend all day thinking about bad clouds?

First of all, you've probably never labelled a cloud as 'bad'. Understand that judgement plays a major role in any struggle with thoughts or feelings. You can choose to label a thought or a feeling as 'bad' in the same way that you can label a cloud as 'bad'.

Cognitive fusion is like attaching a judgement to a cloud and then putting that cloud in charge of your life. If you did that, you'd be constantly checking for bad clouds and, when one appeared, you'd immediately give it all of your time and energy. That cloud in the sky would control your mood. You'd believe it means things about you. You'd do everything you could think of to get rid of it. But the more you kept your attention on that bad cloud, the more you'd notice other nasty clouds around it, and your entire day would get consumed by clouds. You'd become so focused on trying to control the clouds you hate that it would be like standing in a fog, unable to look past the clouds you hate so much.

COGNITIVE FUSION

148 The Basics

Cognitive defusion is like standing on the earth, present to everything in your life, with the clouds floating high over your head. You can pay attention to them if you want, or you can choose to give your awareness to anything else – the cars driving by, the voice of your hairdresser, the snow crunching under your boots, the sandwich you're making, the friend that's sharing a difficult secret with you. All of your experiences have equal importance and you can intentionally choose where to give your attention.

COGNITIVE DEFUSION

SO I JUST IGNORE THE THOUGHTS?

Not exactly. Go back to that question I asked about bad clouds: do you spend all day telling yourself to ignore clouds? If you woke up in the morning and you really wanted to not think about clouds because you've been focusing so much on them lately, you could decide not to look outside, not to watch the weather forecast, to wear a wide-brim hat outside so you don't accidentally see any clouds, and you could avoid all small talk to prevent anybody mentioning that it's a cloudy day. No cloud triggers for you!

But what have you placed completely in charge of your life? The clouds. If you want to ignore something, you give that thing incredible power over your life.

With the exception of meteorologists and fishermen, most people practise 'cloud defusion' every day. The clouds are there. You're aware of them. If you want to pay attention to them, you can. But you probably don't invest in actively trying to ignore the clouds. There's nothing wrong with seeing the clouds and acknowledging their existence. It doesn't mean anything about you. You don't have to do something about the clouds if you notice them. Cognitive defusion is about bringing the same practice to your thoughts. The clouds are simply part of the context in which you function.

That IF X THEN Y pattern is at work again when you're afraid that seeing a cloud in the sky means you're going to have a bad day, or having a monster in your head means you're a monstrous person, or whatever conclusions you're drawing about unwanted experiences you're having. When we believe in that pattern, we try to avoid and ignore X because we think that X must mean Y. That's why it's important to break the pattern. If there's a cloud in the sky, there's a cloud in the sky. That's all. You can have that experience and choose to do things you value. If there's a monster in your head, there's a monster in your head. That's all.

But this takes practice. And what better way to practise than to take all of your intrusive thoughts and urges and anxieties and pack them into a car with you and drive them around town? With the next exercise, that's what you'll do.

EXERCISE: Annoying Kids in the Car

It's tough to get up and over the Unhappiness Curve. You'll experience increased levels of anxiety, your brain will try to convince you that you're about to die, the voices in your head will tell you how worthless and incapable you are in very real, meticulously rational arguments, you'll have thoughts about terrible things happening to those you love, and it'll seem as though the physical feelings you hate will not only get worse, but never go away. It's a perfect time to take a road trip (with all of that stuff in your head that you hate).

The exercise I'll share with you here is a way to apply a popular Acceptance and Commitment Therapy metaphor. Steven Hayes describes it in his book, *Get Out of Your Mind and Into Your Life*, as the 'Passengers on the Bus' metaphor.[16] (In Russ Harris's book, *The Happiness Trap* – another great book using ACT techniques I'd recommend checking out – he describes a similar metaphor as 'Demons on the Boat'.[17]) Personally, I find it useful to approach my brain as though it's a bunch of annoying children I'm driving around. Kids are always trying to get treats, they have no grasp of reality, they make stuff up, they don't want to do healthy things, and they cry and whine all of the time for no reason, just like my brain. So I call this the Annoying Kids in a Car exercise. You'll need to drive these screaming toddlers up and over the Unhappiness Curve. Here's how this exercise works:

1. Grab a comfortable seat and close your eyes.
2. Picture yourself driving a car or some other vehicle that you like. Make it a vehicle that reflects your personality in some way. But make sure it has a back seat or two, because . . .

3. You're babysitting a group of rambunctious toddlers today. As you're driving, imagine the vehicle filling up with little kids shouting and screaming about the thoughts and feelings and urges with which you're struggling right now.
4. Hear the little girl screaming that she hates you because you're not good enough, or the little boy crying in shock because you could fail, you could get hurt so badly. Hear the child whining about wanting more cookies. Hear the little kid's panicked shouts about needing to stop and turn around because you have to go back and deal with the past. Whatever it is that's difficult as you're climbing the Unhappiness Curve, imagine that as a little kid in the car with you. Hear it aloud from a little brat.
5. As you're imagining this experience, consider what you value. Yes, there is a load of screaming rascals in the back seat, but you have places to go. Punch that valued direction into your GPS and keep driving. Imagine the environment around you in the direction of your values. What landmarks do you see that help you accept the shouts in the back seat and stay focused on where you're going? You can take these toddlers with you as you drive towards your values. If you react to everything a toddler shouts at you, you'll never get anywhere.
6. Remember that these compulsion urchins are clever. If they see you reacting to them, they'll push your buttons even more. You can't reason with them – they believe in the Easter Bunny and the Tooth Fairy. You can't forcibly try to control them – you might succeed but that'll only trap you in prison. They know you can't do anything to them. But they also can't do anything to you.
7. Try to see that these kids are scared, tired and hurt.

Can you hear them and feel compassion towards them? How would you treat a child that was crying and upset? Can you understand that the things they yell about come from a place of not being able to express clearly the pain they feel? Can you let them cry and shout? Maybe that's what they need to do right now.
8. Keep driving until you've had a good mental workout, noticing when you're distracted by the angry toddlers and then bringing your awareness back to your values and where you're going.

This is a practice that you can bring into your everyday life. Whenever my brain starts catastrophising or throwing anxieties at me or whining about needing to engage in some compulsion, I can always hear that as an angry toddler crying. I can always express compassion to that voice or that image in my head. I know my brain is expressing what it is from a place of fear, but it can trust me. I'm going to help it do something that I know is healthy for both of us.

PART TWO:

The Transformation

STEP 13

Switch the fuel for life from fear to values

As you become more skilled at taming the monster and no longer feed it compulsions, you'll notice that it doesn't hang around you so much anymore. Even when it does show up to beg for compulsions, you don't spend your time feeding it. But you'll probably notice how much you depended on the monster to determine how you acted every second of the day, everywhere in your life. Now you won't have all that fear and anxiety controlling your actions. This presents its own challenges.

Life without fear is terrifying. I remember very clearly the first time I noticed I wasn't anxious about anything – it was one of the scariest experiences of my life.

One morning, several months after I'd finished working with my therapists and as I continued to cut out compulsions on my own, I was walking down the path behind my apartment building, on my way to a class. The sun shone through the leaves of the trees along the path and lit it up in this soft green glow. The temperature was perfect. It was beautiful. And then a worry popped into my head about people discovering I'd spent my morning on compulsions.

But I hadn't. I hadn't gone back to check anything. I hadn't done any rituals before I left my apartment. I hadn't spent the morning on my computer and then rushed to get ready at the last second.

I was on my way to a class, there would be a group of people there, and I had nothing to hide from them. I wasn't ashamed of anything. I wasn't worrying about the past or the future.

I began to tingle all over. The waves of a full-blown panic attack started flowing out of every cell in my body. Nothing to worry about meant not having any uncertainties to control.

I had always functioned by reacting to uncertainty and then feeling good about preventing my fears from coming true. I depended on the monster spewing out uncertainties and anxieties and feelings I didn't like so I had direction in life. I washed, I ate, I exercised, I socialised, I worked, I studied, I dated, I did everything imaginable as a reaction to whatever the anxiety monster vomited into my life. I lived only to react. I didn't know how to function without constantly fixing problems.

Without the monster to feed, I had to find a new way to function. If I wanted to build better mental health and, most importantly, sustain it, I had to get an entirely new fuel for even the most basic activities in life. That fuel is my values.

So in this second part of the book, we're going to explore how to transform your life from one that's a reaction to fear and anxiety, to one that's proactively fuelled by your values. Part Two is all about how to live with you in charge of your life instead of the monster.

EVERYTHING IS MENTAL HEALTH

Be holistic about your mental health. By 'holistic' I don't mean light some candles and sprinkle lavender oil around. I mean see the whole system and make changes throughout it. How you work, how you study, how you communicate, how you exercise, how you eat, how you sleep – how you do everything is connected to your mental health.

If you focus only on a few compulsions or situations in which you struggle with emotions you don't like, you are like the guy who goes into the gym to only do exercises for his biceps and spends most of the time trying to find the right angle in the mirrors to snap a picture of himself flexing so he can post it online, #curlsforthegirls.

Being holistic about your mental health is about practising accepting uncertainty throughout your life. If you're somebody, for instance, who experiences a lot of anxiety in relationships because you struggle with uncertainty about whether your partner truly loves you, whether you're good enough for them and if you're better than their previous partners – that might be the uncertainty you most want to learn how to handle. However, that's not independent of how you handle uncertainty throughout your life. Every time you experience uncertainty about health, or finances, or work or your appearance, you'll have an opportunity to change how you accept those uncertainties. Like we discussed in Step 9 on checking compulsions, making changes in those other areas to accept uncertainty and align your actions with your values will help you accept the uncertainties you're experiencing in your relationship.

The values that you set earlier will be your compass. They can help guide you in any situation in life. When you use values to approach life and you ask questions like: 'How can I do what I value in this situation?' 'How can I do things that make me healthy and happy over the long term?' 'How can I contribute to my community in a way that's healthy for me and my community over the long term?', then it becomes very necessary to look at *everything* on an ongoing basis. You're not solving a problem; you're creating your life. That's something you can do in every moment. How will you act as yourself, in a way that aligns with your values, throughout all of the systems in your life?

I'll explore a few examples below of the types of change you might make throughout your life as you switch from a reactive, fear-based approach to a proactive, values-based approach.

Work/school/life balance

There is only life. Wherever you're breathing, that's your life. The concept of work/life balance is absurd. Your life won't start after you finish school, after you find the right person, after you've finished work for the day, after you make enough money, after whatever you think is just over the horizon. Your life is right now. It's everything you do. It's every minute of today. So your values matter wherever you're doing whatever you do during the day. That's your life.

Take some time to consider how your values translate into specific actions at work or at school. The culture around you might be highly focused on compulsions. It might encourage them. Be aware of that. How will you navigate that environment? Instead of reacting to the fear of being fired, or the fear of being disliked or the fear of being responsible for a mistake, how can you work proactively to build and create what matters to you?

One way you may find that a values-based approach manifests itself in your work is in the ability to say 'no'. When you react to fear, it's easy to take on more work than you can do because you're afraid of saying 'no' to a colleague or your boss. Or you might agree to act in a way that isn't aligned with your values because you don't see anybody else refusing to do it. You're afraid of what people will say about you if you refuse. Acting according to your values is about standing up for what you believe in. When you make decisions based on your values, the opportunities to say 'no' and the benefits of doing that become much clearer. You're practising being yourself. It's OK if your fears come true, because you're building something stronger and more fulfilling.

Your values can't be something you set aside in your professional life and then hope to use in the few hours of the day when you're not working or studying. Your practice is wherever you're breathing.

Social media

How you use social media and the internet, in general, can either be a way to practise your values or it can be about practising misery and encouraging your brain to give you even more uncertainties and urges to chase after.

It shouldn't be surprising that we can make our mental health worse online. Imagine if you engaged in the same behaviours you engage in online, but you did them in the real world – you followed your friends around, judging how they looked and what they ate, or you spent hours each day stalking a model and judging yourself for not being as muscular and as rich as him, or you ran around listening to conversations and then shouted abuse at anybody you disagreed with, or whenever you did anything you had to ask everybody you saw if they liked what you did, if they wanted to tell others about it, because your self-esteem was entirely dependent on their reactions.

If you did those things in real life, I don't think anybody would be surprised if you ended up a miserable, anxious wreck. You'd probably get thrown in jail, too. It's no wonder that people question if there's a link between social media and poor mental health. But it's not social media that's the problem – it's what you do on it.

Your time on social media can be time spent on things you value. Look at how you've been spending time online. As you make the switch to a value-fuelled life, you're probably going to make big changes in how and what you do. How will your values translate into your actions online?

One of the biggest shifts you might make is from getting to giving. If we go online to get likes, or get reassurance or get relief, that's all about us trying to take from other people. We want to get stuff. It's very selfish. You'll probably find it more fulfilling to redirect your online activities around giving. How do you give support to your friends or to strangers? How do you make others feel happy or lucky? How can you give people useful information?

When you make the shift from getting to giving, you bring success close to you. When you've finished giving what you came to give, you can go and do something else. You've acted in line with your values and you have finished now. If you go online to get things, social media becomes a bottomless pit. You'll dig for ever in search of what you're lacking.

Clothes and grooming

This can be one of the trickiest to change because we're bombarded by messages that we dress and take care of our appearance only to control what others think about us, to avoid embarrassment, to look sexy, to avoid exclusion. But that's guaranteed to make you anxious (and buy more clothes and more make-up, which is why we're fed those messages). Shifting from that approach to one that is based on caring for your appearance as an expression of yourself is liberating. You might think that not focusing on what others think about how you look would lead to you not looking after yourself, but you'll discover you take much better care of yourself.

When I only cared about myself as a means to control what others thought about me, if I didn't plan on seeing anybody that day or I wasn't looking to date anybody, my appearance and self-care would quickly go downhill. I only cared about myself when I felt anxiety about what others might think. How I dressed, groomed and cleaned was entirely fuelled by anxiety. Don't get stuck in that trap. Identify how you want to care for yourself (for you) and stick with that. If there are particular activities you enjoy doing to care for your body, make them part of your Awesome Schedule (see page 168).

When you get dressed in the morning, watch out for turning that into rumination practice time. Can you get dressed as an expression of yourself, not as an attempt to avoid fears or control other people? When you're shaving, washing, or doing any one of the millions of grooming activities we do, can you make that about caring for yourself and appreciating your body instead of trying to solve problems or fight smells or hate being human? This is an opportunity to practise appreciating yourself and showing your brain that your value doesn't fluctuate according to what you think others think about you.

Relationships

Romantic relationships are all about navigating uncertainty. Instead of asking somebody out on a date, it might be more appropriate to ask them if they'd like to join in a threesome with you and a hot, steamy mess of uncertainty. You can all hold hands while experiencing life's wondrous unknowables together.

Craving certainty in a relationship and trying to control yourself or manipulate your partner as a reaction to uncertainty can quickly break apart a relationship. Instead, take time individually, and with your partner, to articulate what matters to each of you in a relationship. What are the values of your relationship? How does each of your individual values translate into shared values and actions? Then put your time and energy into building that relationship you want to see.

You can't know for certain if your partner loves you, or whether they're the right person for you, or whether this relationship will last. What you can know is whether you're giving to the relationship, in this moment, in a way that aligns with your values.

Shifting the focus to values can also help with getting out of bad relationships, especially if we're staying in those bad relationships because we're afraid of what could happen if we leave. If we're reacting to the fear of being alone, or unloved or not valued, or the fear of hurting somebody, it's easy to make decisions in reaction to those fears that only cause more pain for ourselves, as with any compulsion. But if you're looking at whether you can build a relationship with this person in a way that's aligned with your values, then the conversation is very different.

Cleaning

When I'm talking about cleaning here, I mean it in all forms – cleaning yourself, objects, rooms, whatever. Most of us spend a significant amount of time cleaning. You can use that time as an opportunity to practise building better mental health, or you can make it an opportunity to train your brain to react to fear.

Compulsively cleaning is a stereotypical OCD symptom, but I didn't start doing it until my mental health challenges were relatively severe. For me, it was very focused on hand-washing. I'd wash my hands and, a few minutes later, I'd question if I'd washed them well enough or washed them at all. Then I'd go back and wash them again. If I touched things I thought might be 'contaminated', I had to wash my hands quickly before touching anything else. I would also wash my hands under scalding hot water because I wanted to feel the pain so I could be certain I'd killed off all the flesh-eating bacteria or Ebola or whatever it was I was afraid of that day. I didn't want to spread that contamination to somebody else and be responsible for hurting them. You can see that IF X THEN Y pattern at work there again: IF X (my hands aren't in pain) THEN Y (they're not clean and I need to clean them again) and IF X (I'm not perfectly clean) THEN Y (I'll spread a disease to somebody and kill them and everybody will hate me).

In a subtler way, that IF X THEN Y pattern was at work whenever I cleaned my home, because I only cleaned as a reaction to the fear of being judged by others. That might seem normal but it's the type of normal practice that trains the brain to be constantly worrying and afraid. If I only clean when I'm afraid or anxious, it makes anxiety necessary for action. That's not a useful approach to choose if you don't like anxiety.

Whether it's hand-washing or cleaning your home, do it for you and do it proactively because it's an action you value. Revisit the values you articulated earlier and see if caring for yourself and your home fit in there somewhere. If not, you might want to add a value. You don't have to wash your hands because you're trying to control the future. You can wash your hands as a way of appreciating your body. You don't have to clean your kitchen as an attempt to control the thoughts of others. You can clean your kitchen because you're grateful for the help it provides you, or simply because it's a thing you do.

As you wash and clean, it's an opportunity to incorporate your mindfulness skills into your daily life. Keep your mind with you and open up your awareness to your senses – the smell of the soap, the motion of your hands as you wipe the counter, the shine of a clean stove top, all in the present.

DON'T GO BACK TO NORMAL

When somebody says, 'I know it's just the bipolar talking when I want to find a hook-up . . .', or 'I can usually tell when it's a delusional thought . . .', or 'my anxiety is about social situations . . .', it misses the much broader role that mental health plays in their lives. Our mental health challenges are more than the specific problems we see poking up out of the fog of our everyday lives. Yes, there are particular symptoms that you can judge and label, but those are like the peaks in a mountain range. Label them, plant your flag on them if you want, but remember that the peaks are held up by much larger foundations. If the Himalayas are in your way, knocking the top off Mount Everest to make it a more normal-sized mountain only removes a label. You still have a massive wall of rock in your way. Your unique and noticeable symptoms rest on a foundation of totally average, normal practices.

People often tell me they 'just want to be normal again'. They want to 'go back to the way it was when things were normal'. And I cannot emphasise enough how important it is to not go back to the way things were. Do not go back to what you thought of as 'normal'. Normal got you here. Remember that guy from Step 6 who kept jumping in the pool and hated being wet? Don't be that guy.

I don't recommend normal to anyone. It's just like with physical fitness – there might have been a time when you could eat whatever you wanted, drink whatever you wanted and you didn't have to exercise, and everything worked fine and it was no problem. That was normal. And that practice, over the years, very naturally leads to being out of shape. With mental health, you may have spent many years engaging in compulsions and believed that they 'worked'. They did provide short-term relief. You loved feeling certain. Your anxiety monster was cute and quirky. You could take it everywhere. You could joke about it! I understand that completely. Looking back now, I can see that I was working my way up to a mental illness from a very young age. One of my earliest memories that I can recall clearly is from a week I spent one summer constantly ruminating about whether I'd damaged some furniture at a friend's house. From the moment I woke up until I went to bed, that's all I thought about, for days. Every time the phone rang, I was sure it was this kid's parents calling my parents to report what I'd done. Every time I saw that kid, I checked to see if he was angry with me. What if he'd been punished for what I'd done?! He would hate me for ever (although I'd be relieved he got punished instead of me).

For decades, my normal was nothing but coping, checking and controlling compulsions. In amongst all the other compulsions, I continued with that practice of spending entire weeks worrying about horrible things I thought I'd done. I became very skilled at doing all of that 'normal' stuff while also doing well at school, getting good jobs, developing great friendships. I thought my normal worked incredibly well, and I had the rewards from society to prove that my normal was perfectly fine. It was not.

Struggling with mental health is normal. When charities conduct mental health awareness campaigns, they like to talk about research that shows that 1 in 5 people will experience a mental illness in a given year.[18] But that's only the number of people around you right now struggling with full-blown mental illness. The lifetime prevalence is much higher. A Harvard study that did face-to-face interviews with over 9000 people estimated the lifetime prevalence of experiencing a mental illness at 46.4 per cent.[19] That's nearly half the population. It doesn't get much more normal than that. And it's not like the other 53.6 per cent of the population has perfect mental health.

Normal people don't have great mental health, just like normal people don't have great physical health. Struggling with physical health is normal. If somebody is in great physical shape, it's probably because they do not do the same things that the average person does. They do not act normal. And if you don't want to go back to struggling with your mental health, I don't suggest you pursue normal, either.

If any of the changes I've mentioned so far don't sound normal to you, well you're damn right they're not normal.

BUT IF WE DON'T REACT TO FEAR, WON'T EVERYBODY JUST DO WHATEVER THEY WANT?

The premise of this worry is essentially that we'll all become bank robbers and murderers the moment we overcome our fears, because only the fear of punishment or guilt is holding you back from killing whoever stole your lunch from the office fridge.

You may have many anxieties about doing terrible things or being judged by others, and you might believe that your fear of doing those things is actually good for you and helps you. Through improving your mental health, you can learn to experience incredible amounts of anxiety, to immerse yourself in the depths of guilt, to overcome your fear of death, and to achieve all manner of other feats of emotional awesomeness. Fear no longer traps you in a limiting cage. It no longer decides where you can go and what you can do.

With that freedom comes responsibility. You can practise trusting yourself with that responsibility. This is why it's so important to let your values fuel your actions. Feel empowered by that opportunity. You can proactively make choices for yourself and those around you, not out of fear but because you want to live. You don't need fear to control you. This may be difficult to imagine right now but our natural inclination, when fear is not in control, is to do good.

When I spoke to Dr Steven Hayes while I was writing this book, we talked about this topic and he told me that when people are 'healthy and whole, it turns out, they want to create and help others. They want to live and love. They want to dance and contribute and plant and eat and create and grow and change.'

It is so true. I hope you get to do all of that and so much more.

STICKING TO VALUES IS DIFFICULT, BUT MENTAL ILLNESS IS MORE DIFFICULT

Switching to a values-based approach is difficult. You'll catch yourself doing things you don't value all the time. You'll end up lying on your bed, holding your phone in front of your nose watching cat videos, and then suddenly realise you've lost two hours staring at moving lights again. That's normal.

When you catch yourself mindlessly flipping through websites on your phone, recognise that it's happening. You can make a choice about how you want to spend your time.

I love writing and doing creative things in my free time. In the past I would say I didn't have enough time to do what I loved and I'd get upset about that. I'd get very agitated if anybody interfered with my time. I was terrified of not accomplishing all the things I wanted to do and that only fuelled more compulsions as a reaction to the fear of death. But I had lots of time. I simply spent it on things that didn't matter to me. Now I can recognise when I'm starting to put time into things I don't value and I can choose to put my time into something I do value. I can see that I'm about to waste an hour flipping through videos online and I can choose to spend that time with people I care about, or cooking something healthy for dinner.

This is an extension of our mindfulness practice. We notice when we've wandered off to do things we don't value and then we come back to our practice. Ronit Jinich often reminds me during a meditation session that: 'Returning is the practice.' Your values will help you return to the path in your own life.

A big help in returning to an action that's aligned with your values is knowing what those actions are, and knowing how you can engage in everyday actions in a way that's not dependent on anxiety. This next exercise will help you to articulate those actions.

EXERCISE: **The Switch List**

This exercise is all about understanding how you can switch from a fear-based approach to a values-based approach with everyday activities. Apply everything you've learned in the book so far to making these changes: you're going to let yourself experience feelings, you're not going to engage in compulsions, you're going to act proactively instead of reactively, you're going to act in line with your values.

1. Grab a piece of paper and draw a line down the middle. At the top of the paper, on one side, write 'fear-based'. At the top of the paper on the other side of the line, write 'values-based'.
2. In the 'fear-based' column write some of the compulsions you engage in as a reaction to various fears. List compulsions that involve behaviours you'll keep in your life. There are some examples in the table below if you need some suggestions.
3. In the 'values-based' column, write how you'll do that same action but reframe it so that it's proactively helping you move towards what you value.
4. Put these changes into action using tools we've already explored. You can add them into your Hierarchy, for instance. You might pick a week coming up as the week you'll challenge yourself to only open

your email when you have an email to send. Or there might be specific activities you can incorporate into your Awesome Schedule. Perhaps, in the past, you only exercised because the summer was coming, but now you'll make exercise a regular part of your life, not dependent on reacting to the fear of impending public disrobement.

Here are some more examples of making the switch from fear-based to values-based actions:

FEAR-BASED		VALUES-BASED
Dieting because I hate how I look.	→	Eating to fuel my running practice.
Moving to a new city to avoid all the memories that this one triggers and because 'I just want to get away from it all'.	→	Living in a place that's optimal for doing things I value in life.
Sending messages to my partner to get a quick response so I know she cares about me.	→	Sending messages to express to my partner how much I care about her.
Cleaning my home because I'm afraid of getting judged by visitors.	→	Cleaning my home because I care about the place in which I live.
Getting something on my CV because I'm afraid people won't respect me if I don't have the right title or degree.	→	Doing things that have value to my community or my profession.
Showering to avoid feeling contaminated.	→	Showering to care for and appreciate my body.
Helping a customer because I'll get fired if I don't.	→	Helping a customer because I want to support people in the same way I like to be supported.

Avoiding my friends because I don't feel like myself today.	→	Spending time with my friends because that's an action that reflects my values.
Posting a comment online to correct somebody who I believe is wrong.	→	Creating something of use to people and posting that online.
Meditating as an attempt to escape feelings I don't like.	→	Meditating to practise accepting totally natural human experiences.

IN ANY MOMENT YOU CAN RETURN TO THE PRACTICE OF BEING YOURSELF

STEP 14

Break your motivation addiction

I'll admit, you have a lot of work to do. You've started meditating, eliminating the compulsions in your life, doing more of the things you actually care about, letting yourself have feelings you've avoided for years, making changes at work, in relationships, how you use the internet, how you eat, how you exercise – and we're not done yet. There's more work coming up in the steps ahead. Building better mental health takes work, like building better physical health. So you might be wondering how you'll motivate yourself to make all of the changes we've explored.

My recommendation is: don't.

MOTIVATION IS A UNICORN FART

We all know what a unicorn looks like: a horse with a single horn in the middle of its head. It might be flying through the air, or glittering in a magical forest glade, or it might have rainbows streaming out of its tail – there are boundless variations on the precise characteristics of a unicorn, but a child could draw four lines jutting out from the bottom of a round blob, a rectangle pointing upwards at an angle from one side of the blob, an oval on top of that rectangle and a triangle pointing up from that oval and you could probably guess that it's a picture of a unicorn.

What if motivation is similar? We can all describe it, we generally agree on the characteristics that define it, and you can tell somebody that you felt motivated and they'll know what that means based on what they attach that label to in their own head.

But I'd say motivation is even less real than a unicorn. Motivation is a unicorn fart. It's the by-product of a bunch of other imaginary things. You get praise, you get your self-esteem up, you reassure yourself, you throw in some affirmations, you judge your internal experience as good, and then you believe you can do anything you want.

MOTIVATION

That's fine when the feeling's there, but we need to be capable of caring for ourselves even when we don't judge ourselves to be 'motivated'. If you feel motivated to make the healthy changes that need to happen and you can sustain that, then carry on. But if you're like me and you get so motivated to do *everything* and you're incredibly productive for a period of time ... but subsequently don't feel motivated so you don't do anything, then I'd suggest doing away with the idea of motivation completely. You don't need it. It'll only become another barrier, another feeling to chase. You'll end up constantly judging your feelings to check if you feel motivated enough to do what you need to do. Since motivation is the feeling you want, your brain will make you not feel it so you can keep trying to chase it.

Motivation is like every other feeling we've talked about. You can see that IF X THEN Y dependency at work again. IF X (I don't feel motivated) THEN Y (I can't study). It's the same as IF X (I don't feel calm) THEN Y (I can't talk to people). Judging feelings and then reacting to them is what we're moving away from here. You already know where that practice leads.

Let's look at some supports that can help you succeed at making change happen. After that we'll explore something that often trips people up when they're making big changes.

MAKE CHANGE VISIBLE, TANGIBLE AND CONSEQUENTIAL

I once asked Tom Wujec how he helps people overcome all of the assumptions, beliefs, fears, and all the other experiences and emotions that get in the way of change, and Tom very quickly answered: 'You get it out of them.'

In Tom's work helping teams solve wicked problems, a core principle he emphasises is always to make ideas visible, tangible and consequential. That's why we've done exercises like the Compulsion Journey (page 98). That's an exercise you can go back to if you're finding it difficult to make changes in your life. See why it's difficult and see where you can make changes.

Experiment with this approach of making the stuff in your head visible. It'll keep coming up, for example in the next step on beliefs and desires, when you'll get your beliefs out of your head and down on to sticky notes, but go beyond what I suggest. Just keep pulling things out of your head and making them tangible. As Tom explained to me, 'The act of externalising thoughts – putting things into symbols that are understandable – forces a clarifying function.'

Make changes clear. Get them out of the fuzziness of your head. Do this with any change. Here's what that might look like for you: let's say you want to start exercising more. So we want to make that change visible. You need to see it outside your head, which probably means writing it down somewhere. But don't stop there. Making it visible isn't always enough. The number of people who love making lists of things they want to do is far greater than the number of people who actually do any of the things on those lists.

The next thing we want to do with this idea is to make it tangible. At the very least, that'll mean writing down the change on something that's physical and movable. Maybe you write a note that says, 'Go to the gym when you wake up!' and then stick it on your alarm clock, so you have to pick up the note to turn off your alarm.

One of my favourite ways to make an idea tangible is to get an object related to that change and place it in my way. So you might do that by getting your gym clothes ready the night before and putting them right by the door. Make it so you have to step over them. Stick a note on them, too.

Making it consequential is about making these visible, tangible expressions lead to action. To help yourself with that, make sure your reminders are specific. 'Leave for the gym at 6.30' is a better note than 'Go to the gym'. Remove the wriggle room. If you struggle with change, you know your brain is going to exploit every ambiguity it can to reason its way out of it.

You can also introduce some added benefits to going to the gym. Coordinate with a friend to meet at the gym at the same time. Then you get the added benefit of supporting your friend. Not going also has consequences then.

Making it consequential is also about being aware of how the change aligns with your values. This isn't a random change you're trying to force yourself into. If you don't make this change happen, you're missing out on doing what you actually care about in life. Making this change happen is about being you, it's about being happy and healthy.

KEEP SUCCESS CLOSE TO YOU

You can support yourself with making change all you want but the changes you pursue still matter. Always keep in mind what we talked about at the very beginning of the book about goals and goal-setting: keep goals creative and human. I'm going to expand on that here and suggest that you keep goals close to you and achievable. Even for changes that will take a long time to realise – recovery from an illness, building a business, getting a university degree, becoming a professional sports player, raising a family – bring success into the daily practice of taking steps towards those long-term goals.

For instance, if you want to be a successful musician but you're not currently, that's a goal that's far off. Many things need to happen for you to reach that goal. It's going to involve complex changes in your life while navigating a variety of external factors. We want to turn that into something you can actually do today. What you can do today is practise your musical skills. If you practised, then you have been successful today. If you challenged yourself to use skills you're struggling to master, then you have been successful. If you sought help from a teacher to learn about a new technique you can utilise, then you have been successful. Measure success by the actions that lead to the outcome you want. That outcome simply becomes a natural side-effect of your actions in the present.

Personally, I like to keep success extremely close to me. For me, success is breathing. If I take a breath mindfully, then I've been very successful. All of the practices throughout this book are built on that foundation of mindfulness. So my success is all about a support that I find very useful for doing what I value. Because success is so close to me, it also means that, in each moment, I can make my next decision from a position of success. I am successful already, so what's the next step I can take to put that success to use in a way that matters to me? Instead of chasing success, I get to spend it.

It seems that we often want people to chase success, but when we're struggling with something like anxiety, we're always chasing things – calm, relief, reassurance, certainty, a way out, the past, recognition – and that puts us in a position of constantly lacking.

While acknowledging that any change is a process (and is often a very long journey), instead of pursuing the outcome of the change, pursue the immediate steps. You're successful with each step. Celebrate those steps. Continually take successful steps and you'll end up much more quickly in the place you want to be.

DON'T GET FOOLED BY ADDICT MATHS

The thing most likely to get in the way of making a change in your life is your own brain. Not feeling motivated isn't so much about not having a feeling. It's about our brains coming up with wonderfully logical reasons to not make changes we want to make and instead to fall back on what we've done before. I call this 'addict maths'.

You're practising it when you're trying to start a meditation practice but, as you're walking home from work, it begins to rain, and you get upset because you wanted to go to the park to meditate. You prefer to meditate in the park because it feels calmer – it's so Zen! There's too many distractions around your house. But now the park isn't an option. Your favourite meditation bench will be all wet. Although maybe this isn't such a bad thing because it's a Friday night and people are supposed to do fun things on Fridays, right? You've been meaning to meditate all week and you haven't done it yet so what's another day? Isn't meditation more of a Saturday morning type of thing, anyway? Maybe the weather will be nice tomorrow so you can meditate in the park then. And you'll be able to meditate for longer because you won't be as stressed as you are right now after such a long week.

The only problem is that when you get home, you remember you don't have any food in the house. You wanted to pick up groceries at a place near the park after you had finished meditating so you could make dinner. Now that you're home, you don't feel like going back outside into the rain to walk to the store. You need to relax after a stressful week! And why isn't somebody taking you out for dinner tonight?

You start flipping through your dating profiles because you'd really like to meet somebody and start a relationship so you don't have to eat alone anymore. But there's always something wrong with each profile you look at. Nobody fits the criteria of the person you want to date. Dating is so frustrating! You wish you could be in a relationship like this couple in the TV series you've been binge watching. Come to think of it, you really want to know how it ends and you've only got a few episodes left. Until you finish the entire series, it'll keep nagging at you in the back of your head and you won't be able to focus on any of the other things you need to get done. So why not just order a takeaway, crack open a bottle of wine and finish off the series? You were trying to stop eating takeaways every night and start cooking healthier meals for yourself but you do need to eat something. It's true that you decided a couple of months ago that you'd only drink when you were with other people but you were in a serious relationship then. You didn't count on how tough being single would be. You don't need other people to give you permission to do something you want to do. This'll just be one night of indulgence to relax after a long week. Meditating and cooking can wait until tomorrow.

That's addict maths. Your brilliant, debate-winning brain can take the tiniest disruption to your plans and spin it into an equation that sends you right back to where you don't want to be.

The skills and concepts we explored in Part One will help you get around your brain's arguments. You can accept the stuff in your head and stick to your values instead of engaging in coping or controlling compulsions as a reaction to feelings you don't like. Those feelings give you an opportunity to practise mindfulness. It's OK to feel stressed. You don't have to put that feeling in charge of your life. You can break that IF X THEN Y pattern – brains love to use that when they're engaging in addict maths: IF X (it's raining)

THEN Y (I can't meditate). Meditate somewhere else. Get the groceries anyway. Keep that focus on what's important to you over the long term.

If you notice that you're struggling to do the things you actually want to do, that's where you can use the Compulsion Journey exercise on page 98 to explore the complete system around those changes. If you're arriving at the end of the work week so exhausted that you can't seem to stop yourself from crashing into a weekend blur of unhappiness and frustration, what changes can you make earlier in the week, at work or at home? The crash at the end of the week is the symptom, not the problem.

There's also one approach that I've found immensely helpful in implementing change in my life and applying all of the skills we've covered. I'll share that with you . . .

BE UNREASONABLE

You'll always be able to think of a reason to not get out of bed in the morning. You'll always be able to think of a reason to not speak with that person you really want to meet. You'll always be able to think of a reason why exercising is for other people. You'll always be able to think of a reason why the anxieties you're experiencing this time are different, why they seem more legitimate and real, so you should react to them. You'll always be able to think of a reason why today is different and tomorrow is a much better day to get started on doing healthy things. You'll always be able to think of a reason. You're good at thinking.

If you could rationalise and reason your way to better mental health, you would have done it by now. You've thought about it enough.

There's definitely an aspect to building better mental health that's about accepting uncertainty, acting in a way that's aligned with your values and not engaging in compulsions, simply because that's what you do. It's like getting in shape to run a 5K race. You can come up with reasons not to do the training. You can always make a convincing argument as to why you don't feel like going for a run this morning, or why you don't need to eat to fuel your practice, or that you don't need to do any stretching and recovery work. You might come up with very logical arguments. That's great. But do you want to run the 5K race or not?

Making healthy changes requires some unreasonableness.

If you engage in a debate with fear and uncertainty and the urges swirling inside you, they'll always win. The immediate pay-off of reacting to that fear, to eliminating that uncertainty, to finding relief, will always seem to make more sense than sticking to your values and making a decision that's best for you and those around you over the long term. When faced with that angry monster we talked about, it only seems to make sense to give it what it wants so it'll leave you alone.

Be brave and unreasonably healthy. Kiss the monster. Tickle it under its chin. Do what you know will make you happy and healthy over the long term because it's what you do.

CAN I DO THIS ON MY OWN?

Maybe. Maybe not.

Committing unreasonably to health is as much about going when you think you should stop as it is about stopping when you think you should go. A runner who pushes on through pain could injure themselves so badly they won't be able to run anymore. So get help. In the Introduction, I mentioned getting some support, such as connecting with a psychologist or a peer support worker to help guide you on this journey. Sometimes it's not motivation we need but somebody with awareness of the path ahead gently pushing us to take the next step forward.

Working with an experienced professional for your mental health and fitness will be as useful as working with an experienced professional for your physical health and fitness. Look for somebody who knows what works because they live it and they demonstrate that experience. You probably wouldn't want a fitness trainer who's not in great physical shape – how are they going to help you make the changes necessary to live a healthy lifestyle if they can't overcome those challenges themselves? The same is true with mental health.

Many people before you have walked the path you're taking. Talk to them. Learn from them. They're not going to know everything that'll happen, but they'll know where many of the hazards are on your path. There's no benefit to stepping in quicksand because you didn't want to get help when any number of mental health adventurers could have told you, 'Oh yeah, don't go that way; you'll get stuck in quicksand.' They can help you find a healthy path that you can stay on even when your brain is screaming at you to fall back into your old compulsions.

I wouldn't be where I am now if I hadn't chosen to stop listening to my own brain and start listening to other people's brains. You can try to do this on your own through trial and error, but if your approach in the past has only led to more mental health challenges, then it's possible you'll approach this challenge in the same way. Remember: normal got you here. If you want to get out of the place you're in right now, you're not going to use the brain that only knows how to be in that place.

This might all seem a bit counter-intuitive. You need to practise breaking the motivation addiction. The next exercise will help with developing the skills to do just that.

EXERCISE: **Practise Not Feeling Right**

When learning how to do things you don't feel like doing, as with any exercise, start small. Don't try forcing yourself to make some massive change before you've learned how to make small changes – your head will explode. Instead, bring your awareness to the countless times throughout each day when you put uncomfortable feelings in charge of your life. When you avoid stepping out your door because you hear somebody outside and you don't want to have an awkward conversation with them. When you're in the middle of studying but pull out your phone to check your dating app for messages. When you drop something on the floor and don't pick it up because you can always do it later and it's somebody else's job to take care of that, anyway. Those are opportunities to experience uncomfortable feelings, accept that they're there, but not to let them control your actions.

I'll list some examples of how to do this exercise but adapt to what makes sense in your life. What feelings are you training your brain to avoid? When you encounter that resistance, push into it.

- **Wash your laundry before you absolutely must do it.** Yes, you could leave it until later in the week. There are probably other things you'd much rather do today. You have a clean(ish) pair of boxers somewhere that'll get you through tomorrow. But this is just another way we wait for pressure to build up. We train our brains to only act when the pressure is unbearable. Show your brain that misery need not be a prerequisite for action. Do your damn laundry.
- **Respond to messages when you don't feel like responding.** How often have you put off writing an email or a message because you didn't feel you were in the right mood or prepared enough to respond? Show your brain that you can write as yourself while you feel anything. Consider your values and write aligned with them. Incorporate this with the checking challenge we covered earlier (page 111) – send messages when you don't feel like it, without checking them over.

- **Try (not) saying something.** If you notice that you dislike silences and you often speak to fill them, or you often judge what people are saying as incorrect or critical of you and you feel the need to speak up and correct them, try not saying something next time. Are you creating something with your comments or are you trying to relieve a feeling you don't like? Are you only trying to control people to cover up your own insecurities?

  On the other hand, if you're somebody who often doesn't speak up because you feel uncomfortable talking, or you judge yourself, or you notice that you later regret not standing up for yourself in difficult situations, then practise speaking up. Your silence will only create more suffering.
- **Eat a food you hate.** This is an opportunity to explore why you dislike something. Pick a food that might be useful for you to eat regularly. Try eating it mindfully. Be present to all of the experiences you have as you prepare the food and then eat it. Can you appreciate the food and all of the work that went into getting it to you? Can you like the taste? Where does the dislike come from? Can this food become part of your life?
- **Initiate conversations.** You might see a person you know but you're worried you've forgotten their name, or you're not sure if they've noticed you yet, or if they even want to speak to you, so you hold back and pretend that you haven't noticed them. Don't wait for them to make eye contact with you or to make the first move. You can interact with people. Those feelings and uncertainties can be there. It doesn't matter if you're an introvert or an extrovert. Talking is like using a knife – it's a skill. Introverts can be skilled at talking, too.

We stumble over these tiny patches of feelings we don't like as we interact with the world, swirling around and through us. Find those moments, notice your attempts to cope and check and control, and go against them in a way that'll be healthy for you and those around you. Add these exercises to your Hierarchy (page 84) so you can practise in a structured way. You might decide that for a week you're going to practise initiating conversations with people you sit next to on the bus to work. They don't have to be 'good' conversations and people may not want to talk to you. That's totally fine. Like we talked about with success, keep the goal close to you. If you tried to initiate a conversation and that's what you're practising this week, you were successful. Keep practising. You'll sweat, you'll push yourself, you'll fail, you'll try again, it'll get easier.

MAKE SUCCESS POSSIBLE NOW

STEP 15

Throw out unhelpful beliefs and desires

> 'In order to overcome my fear of having a panic attack on an airplane so I could fly to Cabo San Lucas, I had to change what I wanted. In the past all I wanted was to not experience anxiety or panic during a flight. Now my goal was to make it to Cabo dead or alive. Cabo was awesome.'
>
> Anthony

My long-running dedication to paranoia started when I was quite young. One of my earliest paranoid memories is of hiding presents under my bed at Christmas time – not the presents I was giving, but the presents other people gave me. I did this from when I was a little kid, well into adulthood. I hid the presents under there because I knew thieves were watching our house and, when my family and I went off to visit our relatives, the thieves would break in and take everything. I hid some of the presents under the corner of my bed I thought the thieves would be least likely to look under, and I hid the most valuable stuff under the duvet or under my pillows because, let's be honest, smart thieves will look under the bed, but will they look under my pillows?

I would spend the day thinking about the presents and, on the way home, I would imagine how we'd pull into the driveway and the thieves would still be there and then I'd have to fight them.

We've already explored how that paranoid streak continued and expanded as my mental illness struggles worsened – I thought people were trying to poison me, trying to steal everything I owned, they were always spying on me. I was always in danger from something.

The reason I'm mentioning paranoia is because it helped me unravel the much bigger system at work beneath my compulsions. I knew I had to cut out compulsions and I recognised that I was engaging in them as a reaction to fears about getting killed, losing resources and being alone. So I cut out the compulsions one by one. But I still felt this intense pressure to do them. I still believed I was being watched. I still believed my fears would come true and that all of my fears were terrible things I couldn't experience.

I had reasons for everything going on in my head. Even when I was working with my therapists, I never mentioned paranoia as something that bothered me. I never noticed it because I was always drowning in it. But one day, as I was walking into my living room, I felt the urge to walk differently because I was sure I was being watched through the large window that ran the length of the room, and for the first time I really noticed those thoughts. Why did I believe I was being watched?

As I peeled the compulsions away, I found they were only one component of a system for interacting with the world that kept pushing me towards the compulsions and reinforcing unhelpful beliefs. We looked at this system earlier as a linear system, but now let's look at it as a loop with a new component added at the centre: your beliefs (see opposite).

Your beliefs are at the core. There's constant feedback between each node in this system and your beliefs.

Throughout this book, you've been learning skills to make changes in this system and dismantle it. Each time you make a change, it's an opportunity to rewrite beliefs. When you practise mindfulness and sit with an experience without trying to control it, you're also helping yourself change your beliefs about whether or not you can have that experience. Often, those beliefs are what I call 'unhelpful beliefs'. The belief that I was always being watched is an example of one. The more changes you can make in this system, the easier and more sustainable

```
        INTERNAL
          AND
        EXTERNAL
       EXPERIENCES
           ↕
COPING,         JUDGEMENTS
CHECKING,  ↔ BELIEFS ↔
CONTROLLING        ↓
     ↑              UNCERTAINTY,
     |              ANXIETY,
   DESIRES ←    AND OTHER
                     FEELINGS YOU
                     DON'T LIKE
```

your healthy changes will become. If you cut out the compulsions but you don't also throw out the desires, judgements and beliefs that led to them, you'll always find yourself being pushed back into behaviours that cause the same old problems in your life. For instance, if somebody constantly tries to manipulate others into giving them positive feedback by posting questions on social media about their appearance, and they cut out that controlling compulsion but don't get rid of their desire for positive feedback or their belief that their self-worth depends on what others say, they'll only go hunting for a new compulsion to fulfil that desire and align their experience with their beliefs. It's a recipe for repeated disasters.

BREAK OUT OF BAD FLOW

Spiralling around this system is the mirror opposite of being in a state of 'flow'. I call it 'bad flow'. Flow is a concept developed by psychologist Mihály Csíkszentmihályi to describe an optimal state of well-being when people are completely immersed in tasks they enjoy and the level of challenge meets their level of skill. When we struggle with mental health, we get locked into bad flow: a non-optimal state of being where we're completely immersed in tasks that seem to get more and more challenging, taking us further and further from what matters to us. Everything becomes a crisis when you're in bad flow. Even when there aren't any external crises, they're happening inside you.

Cutting out compulsions and doing things you value is a helpful step towards getting into that optimal state of flow in your life. It's also important to tackle beliefs, judgements and desires. Until I dealt with those other components of how I interacted with the world, I was constantly getting pushed into relapse, or at least I felt this never-ending, anxious pressure to relapse and get lost again in that bad flow. Bad flow was easy. It's what I'd practised my entire life. It made me miserable but I was good at it. I struggled to get up and over the unhappiness curve so I kept dropping back on what I'd done before.

In the next step, we'll look at judgements and practising non-judgement. In this step we'll look at how you can make changes with beliefs and desires so you can break out of bad flow.

BELIEFS

It's much easier to throw out unhelpful beliefs than it is to throw out intrusive thoughts, feelings or urges. That's because you can change your beliefs. Once a thought pops into your head, it's already happened. If you're already experiencing it, the only way to not have that experience would be to travel back in time and not feel it in the first place. If you're not a time traveller, it'll be much easier to change your beliefs about those experiences.

If you believe that dying is a terrible thing to be afraid of, you're constantly going to try to judge the danger and possibility of death around you. You'll want to get rid of the feelings caused by those judgements, and so you'll spend all day compulsively trying to cope with, check on, and control your fear of death, worrying about loved ones dying, spending hours researching cancer symptoms online, ingesting an ever-evolving regime of supplements and detoxes to ward off the spectre of old age, and obsessing over items on your bucket list.

Or if you believe you should be a good person and thinking bad thoughts makes you a bad person, that'll lead to constantly judging the stuff in your head, trying to correct thoughts, looking for ways to distract yourself from experiences, chasing after the 'right' kind of meditation to erase the particular issues bothering you, and you'll try to avoid situations in life that trigger the thoughts you dislike, progressively shrinking your life.

Or if you believe your value comes from being liked by others and, in order to be liked, you need to have certain material things and accomplish certain milestones, you'll always be chasing things you don't have, judging yourself, judging how people treat you, and basing your self-worth on those judgements. Society's ideas about attractiveness, status and value are constantly changing, so you'll be stuck in a never-ending battle to control what others think about you.

Those three examples of beliefs don't even begin to scratch the surface of how the beliefs we hold can shape our lives. Critically reflect on the beliefs you hold. Work backwards from your actions to uncover them.

Beliefs are choices. Those choices have natural consequences. If you insist on holding on to beliefs that lead to you damaging your health, that's a natural consequence of those beliefs. If we choose to hold on to the beliefs that lead to us stumbling back into compulsions, then we're choosing to experience the consequences of those compulsions.

If your beliefs aren't working for you, get new ones. It's your brain, after all.

At every node in that system we looked at – experiences, judgements, the feelings you don't like, desires, compulsions – you have an opportunity to rewrite your beliefs when you don't move on to the next node in the system. You can experience the desire to spend all night ruminating about an argument you had with your mother over an email but, instead of engaging in that compulsion, you can let that urge be there in your head while you go and work in the community garden down the street. That helps rewrite your brain's belief about needing to be certain about the argument or solving it in a way that makes you feel certain you were 'right'. Or, further up the system, you can judge an experience and sit mindfully with the feelings created by that judgement, letting them be there. Your actions show your brain that it doesn't need to do something with those feelings. It doesn't have to be afraid of them.

By cutting out compulsions and doing what we value, we start to notice unhelpful beliefs pushing us off-course and getting in the way. We pull back all the layers of assumptions and judgements that have covered up those beliefs for so many years. We accepted them as truth. It might never have occurred to us that they even were beliefs or anything changeable. We existed in them like fish exist in water.

One belief or a set of beliefs you'll probably find useful to change are your beliefs about trust, particularly in yourself. Making the changes we've explored and doing more of what you want in life is much easier if you trust yourself.

SHOW YOUR BRAIN THAT YOU TRUST YOURSELF

Do you trust yourself to do things well the first time? Do you trust yourself to act like yourself in any situation? Do you trust yourself not to forget? Not to screw up? Not to embarrass yourself? Not to choose the wrong partner, or the wrong job, or the wrong option on the menu? Do you trust yourself?

It's through our actions that we can show our brains we trust ourselves. Your brain won't learn this by you telling it that you're trustworthy. You need to show your brain that you trust yourself. That will change the beliefs you hold about trusting yourself.

I certainly thought I trusted myself, but my actions said something completely different. Every time I went back to check, every time I went digging for reassurance online or from people around me, every time I avoided responsibility or social situations, or spent hours ruminating on what to write in an email, and in so many other little actions every day I was telling my brain: 'Don't trust this guy. Worry about what he's done. Don't trust him to handle any problems.'

Do your actions show you trust yourself? Or do you treat yourself like an incompetent employee you need to micromanage and keep away from important tasks?

In the same way that it's difficult to accept uncertainties that trigger intense amounts of anxiety if you don't first learn how to accept less-intense uncertainties, so too will you struggle to trust yourself to handle major life decisions and events if you don't learn to trust yourself with the tiny, everyday decisions that make up your life. After years of teaching your brain not to trust yourself, it's time to make trust a practice.

WHAT'S YOUR TRUST SCORE?

Imagine you have a tiny little bank nestled in your brain. Every time you trust yourself, the teeny bankers in this tiny bank keep track of that. They track it with a trust score. It's like your credit score. Every time you accept uncertainty and do something you value, that adds points to your trust score. Every time you feel gratitude and appreciation towards yourself for taking care of yourself, you add a few more points. And whenever you engage in checking compulsions because of an uncertainty about the past, you knock a few points off. When you engage in controlling compulsions because of your fears about the future, you take more points off. You're telling the bankers: don't trust this person.

When you encounter a big uncertainty that really matters to you – a decision that you believe will impact your life significantly – you go to the banker in your head to borrow the trust you need to make that leap of faith in yourself. But if you've got a negative trust score, that banker isn't going to give you the trust to make that leap. And you'll end up falling back on what you've done before.

If we spend all day practising not trusting ourselves, it's not at all surprising that we don't trust ourselves when we need to the most.

And when I'm talking about trust, I want to emphasise that I don't mean reassuring yourself that your worries won't come true – in other words, trusting that bad things won't happen. That might be what you desire but that's not what I mean by trust. I mean trusting yourself to handle whatever disasters or wonders may come in the future.

DESIRES FOR DISASTERS

It's easy to become overwhelmed by desires. They can swallow up our days and take over our lives. If you desire to be rich but are not well off, you'll need to spend a lot of time and energy becoming rich. If you're afraid that somebody threatens your chances of becoming rich or staying rich, that fear can spark many compulsions to control that uncertainty. Those compulsions can lead to you losing everything you've spent so much time chasing. Ask Macbeth about that one.

On a less Shakespearean scale, you can see desires at work behind any compulsion that fuels poor mental health. Maybe you want to be certain that you didn't do something terrible, or you want to feel safe. You want to know that the person you love, loves you, you want to quieten the shouting in your head, you want to clear your conscience, you want people to respect you, you want acceptance, you want another doughnut, another drink, another hit, another touch, you want to feel happy, you want to prevent people from hurting you, you want to avoid triggering situations, you want to have sex, you want to stop panic attacks, you want to be praised, you want people to like you, you want to avoid being broke, or getting fired, or being hated, or being alone, or maybe you just want to get rid of that constant feeling of anxiety that's always humming through your body, every waking minute.

Many of our desires are about not wanting to feel things. Even with people who experience panic attacks, they may identify a particular situation that brings on their attacks, such as flying or giving speeches, but research shows that for many of those people, it's not the situation they're actually scared of, but the experience of having the panic attack.[20] That's unpleasant. But that desire to avoid the experience leads to the person checking and controlling to make sure it's not happening, which increases their chances of judging something internal or external as a sign that it is happening, which scares them and leads to more attempts to check and control, which leads to it actually happening.

If you want to get rid of anxiety more than anything else in the world, your brain will give you all sorts of things to feel anxious about so you can try to get rid of that feeling and get what you want more than anything else in the world. Your brain is trying to help you. It's giving you the opportunity to get what you want. So be aware of what you desire. If you want nothing more in life than to stop being sad, you will feel sad so you can constantly engage in compulsions to get rid of that feeling. Those compulsions will only lead to you having that experience more, at increasing levels of intensity and complexity. If getting rid of sadness is great, then getting rid of extreme sadness must be even better, right?

SO HOW DO YOU CHANGE A DESIRE?

Well, you don't. It's already there. How could you change it? It'll be more useful to explore how you can handle it, how you can make a mindful decision about what your next step will be. The urge can be there as you take a step towards what actually matters to you.

As your mindfulness practice develops, you can become more aware of desires rising up inside you. They can feel very enjoyable to entertain and chase after. You might want to send a mean email to a co-worker, or maybe quit your job and run off to Thailand in search of yourself, or maybe have one more drink because you deserve it. These are all desires you can have. Like any thought your brain can throw at you, a desire is separate from you. You experience these like any other thoughts or emotions or physical sensations. You can have these experiences, and make a decision aligned with your values.

You don't have to change a desire. There are no right or wrong desires. You can experience any desire in the same way that you can walk past a tree on the street and that doesn't mean anything about you, or that you need to do something about the tree. What matters are your actions.

As you change your actions and align them with your values, instead of reacting to whatever desire pops up, you'll start to rewrite the beliefs in your brain about what you need to do when you experience a desire. Your brain will start to learn that you don't have to react to every urge that hits you.

The Annoying Kids in the Car exercise (page 150) that we went over in Step 12, to help to develop cognitive defusion skills, is a useful exercise to practise with desires. Toddlers want everything! Sometimes we do need to listen to what they want. But if we're driving around chasing after every single one of their whims, we'll never get to travel in a direction that matters to us. You can hear the desires they're shouting from the back seat of the car and you can be empowered to make a decision about where you'll drive. Remember: you control the steering wheel.

Sometimes, however, we're not clear on exactly what our desires are or how they connect to beliefs. You might struggle to even articulate what your beliefs are. So the next exercise is to help get that stuff out of your head and give you some different perspectives on it.

EXERCISE: **Make Your Beliefs Visible**

Back when we were talking about how to make change happen, I mentioned the importance of that principle I learned from Tom Wujec to always make ideas visible, tangible and consequential. We'll be putting that to use here again. We're generally much more capable of understanding complex challenges when we externalise our thinking. You can see this in action any time you write down a maths equation on paper to help you solve it. The equation doesn't change but your ability to solve it does.

Your beliefs are a dynamic component of the unsolvable equations of life. It's entirely possible you've never articulated them before. This is an opportunity to get them out in the open.

1. Grab sticky notes or small pieces of paper and something to write with.
2. Write down what you believe. Write only one belief per sticky note. You need to be able to move them around afterwards.
3. Be as specific as you can, but also look for big, underlying beliefs. So, you might write down some specific beliefs like: 'I believe my husband loves me when he responds to my messages immediately', and 'Getting compliments at work means that I'm valued', as well as some broader beliefs such as 'I need to feel liked'. Get them all out there.
4. Now it gets interesting. I'm not going to tell you anything specific to do with your beliefs. You need to get creative here. But below, I share some ideas on what you can do with them once they're out of your head. The purpose here is to help you shift your perspective, see which beliefs are helpful and which ones aren't,

and begin to recognise that these are changeable, movable ideas. Here are some ideas to explore:

- Try sorting the beliefs. You could move the most problematic ones to the top and the most helpful ones to the bottom.
- Cluster together related beliefs. What do you learn from that?
- Which beliefs are most relevant to your values and which ones seem least relevant?
- Sort the beliefs by which ones are opinions and which ones are facts.
- Which beliefs involve things that are under your control and which involve things not under your control? Cluster them together. How much time do you spend on things not under your control?
- Connect these beliefs to your Inventory (page 34). Which beliefs use up the most time and energy?
- Using the Ideal Inventory as a guide, have you missed any beliefs that you might need to hold if you want to do the things on your Ideal Inventory?
- Sort the beliefs by pain. Put those causing the most pain to the top, those causing the least pain to the bottom.
- Try sorting them on different 2 x 2 matrices to give yourself four quadrants of beliefs. For example, you could do Relationship x Compulsions. That would show you things such as which beliefs are high in relationship significance and high in compulsions, which ones are high in relationship significance and low in compulsions, which ones are low in relationship significance and high in compulsions, and which are low in both. Or, as in the illustration opposite, the beliefs can be sorted by beliefs about the past or future, and by which ones are helpful or unhelpful.

Throw out unhelpful beliefs and desires

HELPFUL BELIEFS ↑

- I'M A GOOD PERSON
- I CAN HELP PEOPLE
- I CAN LEARN FROM MY PAST
- I'M NOT GOOD WITH MONEY
- I NEED TO BE IN CONTROL
- I SHOULDN'T BE ANXIOUS
- I MUST HIDE MY MISTAKES
- PEOPLE ARE ALWAYS JUDGING ME
- I'LL NEVER GET OVER THIS
- NOBODY WOULD LOVE ME IF THEY KNEW ME

↓ **UNHELPFUL BELIEFS**

← ABOUT THE PAST — ABOUT THE FUTURE →

As you go through this exercise, question your assumptions about your beliefs. Be curious instead of judgemental. If you're struggling with your mental health, it's very likely that you're operating with some beliefs that aren't helping you. Get them out of your head and play with them.

STEP 16

Practise non-judgement

> 'No matter what thoughts or emotions my brain throws at me, I recognise them for what they are, and let them be there, surrendering to what is, dropping all judgements, while moving toward my values.'
>
> Scott

I thought of myself as somebody who was very skilled at judging. I was a quick, accurate judge of character. I could tell what type of person you were after seeing a picture of you or reading a few sentences you'd written. I knew everything about everybody I saw on the street. I could spot what was going wrong at work before anybody else was aware of it. I knew when a relationship was over before my partner felt it.

That was all part of the problem.

Judgements are a key component of the practices that push us into poor mental health. Judgement is the spark that detonates all of the feelings that push us into coping, checking and controlling. Life will throw enough challenges at you without you creating more for yourself with your judgements.

To understand how to practise non-judgement, it can help to explore why judgements happen at all. Even if you're the most prolific judger, you already make choices about what you judge, and those choices are wrapped up in your beliefs.

WHY DON'T YOU SPEND ALL DAY JUDGING UGLY PAINT?

Out of the window beside my desk I can see a linden tree across the street. It's one of the tallest trees on the street. It has branches full of green leaves jutting out from the trunk all of the way up. There are thousands of leaves on the tree.

Of those thousands of leaves, some are not perfect. In fact, some are downright ugly. And some are just bad leaves – they're shrivelled, they've got holes, they've turned yellow and stopped all of that wonderful photosynthesising they were doing for the tree.

If you were walking past that tree, why wouldn't you get upset about those leaves? Why wouldn't you spend your day climbing the tree, finding all of the bad leaves, trying to correct them, getting angrier and angrier about them? Why don't you do that with every tree you walk past?

If you did put time into judging the leaves and controlling them, it would be just like judging the clouds in the sky, as we discussed back in Step 12. There are so many things we're surrounded by that we don't give up time and energy to judge every day. You could wake up every morning and immediately begin to judge the paint on the wall in your bedroom. Many people do wake up in the morning and immediately begin to ruminate and obsess about all the things they're worried about. They obsess about what they're obsessing about. They get upset about the feelings of anxiety that swamp them as soon as they open their eyes. But not many people wake up and judge the paint in their room. Why don't you judge the paint? Throughout your day, you probably see many painted walls and some of them are surely ugly shades of peeling, faded, outdated colours. So why don't you devote all your time and energy to fixing all of that ugly paint?

The more you practise mindfulness and meditation, the more you'll find space between you and your internal experiences. It's in that space that you can start to make choices about what you'll do with an experience. You can choose whether to judge it or not. Practising non-judgement doesn't mean you agree with the experience. It doesn't mean you negate the experience. The thought, feeling, or physical sensation is there, like a leaf on a tree, paint on a wall, or a cloud in the sky. It's part of your experience. As you practise cognitive defusion with these experiences and you put some space between you and them, in the gap you'll find beliefs underlying your judgements – beliefs about what should and shouldn't happen, how things should or shouldn't be. Are those beliefs useful to you?

Personally, one of the most interesting areas within which to explore my judgements and to practise non-judgement was with my internal experiences, like emotions and physical sensations.

Our bodies are amazing. Sometimes, they even work relatively well. There's so much going on in them. At this moment, you could judge any number of physical or emotional experiences you're having. There'll be many great experiences and a couple of nasty ones all happening simultaneously. Those experiences are like leaves. You can be aware of them and choose what you want to do with them. But all of those experiences are filtered through your brain. Do you believe what your brain tells you?

I've learned not to believe mine – believing the stuff that comes out of my brain is a one-way ticket to Crazy Town. The challenge is, however, that our perceptions of physical experiences can be very useful to living our lives. If a knife gets too close to your finger and you feel some pain, you can recognise that and pull your finger away so you don't slice it off. In that situation, it's useful to recognise that pain and take action. If you don't, you'll lose a finger. But if you're struggling with emotions and thoughts and other mental experiences you don't like, there's a very good chance you'll also be struggling to handle physical experiences. Through practice, your brain can judge all physical sensations as indicators of imminent danger, triggering anxiety and a fight-or-flight response, whether it's actually useful to you or not. Let's look at some examples.

MISOPHONIA, VOMIT AND PEEING MY PANTS

One of the ways my mental health issues manifested in physical sensations came in the form of what's known as 'misophonia'. Basically, I couldn't tolerate particular sounds. The sounds were physically uncomfortable, and over several years they progressively became unbearable.

One sound I could not stand to be around was the sound of chewing. To this day, even though I can now sit with people chewing loudly and I don't have problems with any sounds, when I recall memories of being around people chewing loudly in the past, my arms tingle and I can feel that panicked urge to get away, just like I would back then. It's seared into my nervous system.

The physical discomfort I experienced from the sounds I hated was an experience I didn't want to have. I didn't believe I could do anything I wanted to do while I experienced that discomfort, so I went out of my way to avoid the sounds I hated. Once the sound was gone, the uncomfortable feeling in my body would dissipate, and I would get on with whatever I was doing. But the more I engaged in those compulsions to avoid and control sounds, the less tolerance I had for them.

This wasn't the only physical experience that challenged me. I hated vomit and all of the physical experiences connected with that. Until I was in my thirties, I did everything humanly possible to avoid eating eggs or oatmeal. That was mostly about the texture, although even the smell of eggs could make me nauseous and feel like I was about to vomit. I hated eggs more than anything else on the planet. Similar to the sounds I avoided, it wasn't an intellectual decision to dislike eggs. My body hated eggs.

I struggled with my perceptions of what was happening in my body. The slightest bit of nausea could trigger worries about vomiting. An odd pain in my side would set me off Googling about cancer or HIV. Before doing anything I thought of as important, such as giving a big presentation, I would go to the toilet multiple times. I truly felt that I did need to pee, badly, and if I didn't go I was convinced I'd have an accident in front of everybody while I was doing the presentation.

The physical sensations I experienced in all of those examples were real experiences. They were as real as experiencing anxiety. Anxiety is a real experience. An image popping into my head of me stabbing somebody is also a real experience. Seeing a leaf on a tree is a real experience. I can choose what I do with these experiences. I can judge them or not. So what did I do?

I practised experiencing them on purpose. I sought out the sounds I hated and experienced the physical reactions to them, recognising that I had flexibility in what I did with those experiences and what meaning I attached to them. I ate eggs every day for a month. That was about showing my brain it was wrong about eggs and vomit. I practised liking the eggs and liking the idea of becoming nauseous and vomiting. If I vomit, that's OK! I can vomit everywhere! I would like nothing more in the morning than to get on the bus and vomit on everybody!

You can see that Acceptance and Commitment Therapy structure there again and the second trick of accepting the consequences.

I stopped going to the toilet before important events when I felt that I needed to go. I started eating again before those events to fuel being myself. I would agree with my brain that I was in desperate need of a toilet and I was going to wet myself. In fact, I would tell myself, I probably already had, and I wasn't going to check. I was going to walk straight into that presentation with a big wet stain on my trousers and introduce myself, smiling to everybody.

TRY CURIOSITY INSTEAD OF JUDGEMENT

In his book *You Are Here*, Thich Nhat Hanh suggests taking a piece of paper and writing on it: 'Are you sure of your perceptions?' and then sticking that on a wall.[21] Grab a sticky note, write it down, and keep it where you can see it because that monster in your head will try anything to get you to feed it compulsions again, including giving you the real physical experiences that terrify you the most.

If you struggle with physical experiences when you're about to do something stressful or new – maybe when you're about to go on a date or volunteer to do something at work you've never done before – try to welcome those with curiosity. Can you let that sensation or that discomfort be there? What does it feel like? Where do you feel it? What anxieties is it triggering? Try going through the Five Whys exercise we covered earlier (page 129). Is your body responding to a fear? What is your body trying to help you prevent by offering you this warning, even if turns out to be a false alarm? What are those annoying kids in the back seat crying about? Are they threatening you with pee on your new car's upholstery because they want to avoid the place you're taking them?

Exploring physical sensations with curiosity is a practice you can then extend to any experience, such as anxiety or the urge to engage in a behaviour you want to cut out. You can be curious about those experiences instead of judging them and triggering the feelings that make compulsions seem necessary.

WILL PRACTISING NON-JUDGEMENT MAKE ME A BAD PERSON?

Non-judgement is the topic about which I receive the most passive-aggressively angry messages. I think it's very misunderstood. Practising non-judgement isn't about practising it to the exclusion of judgement. This is about developing the capacity to have a choice. This is about recognising that running up to every person you see and wrapping them up in labels, before hitting them on the head with all your baggage, isn't the best approach in every situation. This is about giving you freedom – the freedom to create and build what you want to see in your life and your community.

Do you currently have the ability to *not* judge something? Can you meet somebody without judging them? Can you hear a song and hear only the music, not your judgements about that type of music or what it might mean about you to listen to it? Can you feel a physical sensation in your body without judging it as something that shouldn't be there? Can you prevent a bad day from derailing your life? Can you fail? Can you appreciate yourself without grasping after valuables and judging your worth based on them? Can you look in the mirror without seeing a problem to fix?

When you judge a voice in your head as an experience you shouldn't have, when you judge a pain inside you as wrong, when you judge an urge as something that needs relieving, when you judge an error at work as career-ending, when you judge an intrusive thought as blasphemous, when you judge yourself as disgusting, when you judge anxiety as something you shouldn't feel, when you judge your partner as abandoning you because you can see they're online but they're not messaging you ... these all have totally natural outcomes: more struggling and suffering.

Judgement is the first compulsion. The feelings you don't like that arrive after your judgements are totally natural and inevitable. If you want to put an end to those inevitabilities, learn how to practise non-judgement. Give yourself the choice. There's incredible freedom when a thought is a thought, a text message is a text message, your gut is your gut, a car is a car, and you can make decisions based on your values while experiencing whatever you're experiencing.

Practising non-judgement doesn't mean we give up on what we value for ourselves or our communities. Practising non-judgement is part of the transformation from a fear-fuelled life to a values-fuelled life. Practising non-judgement means you're no longer confined by the judgement machinery in your head. It means you can do the things you value, not because you're forced to or it would be wrong not to, but because it's in those actions where you find long-term benefit for yourself and your community.

Give non-judgement a chance. After years becoming an expert judger, it'll be tough at first. But you'll soon find that you have so many other uses for that brain power you're currently pumping into judging everything. Next up are some ways to help you understand how your brain judges and how you can practise non-judgement.

EXERCISE: Non-judgement Practice

If you were performing a complex weightlifting manoeuvre in the gym, you'd break it down into its component movements to help you understand how to do the exercise effectively. We're going to do the same for non-judgement, which is a component of mindfulness and, in a broader sense, a component of learning how to cut out compulsions and do things you value.

There are two things in particular to pay attention to when you're practising non-judgement during the activities coming up:

1. Can you prevent the judgement that triggers the feelings you don't like? It'll be tough at first, but try to develop your understanding of how that judgement happens.
2. When you do judge things, can you choose to do something you value instead of engaging in a compulsion and giving up control of your life to that judgement?

Here are the activities:

1. The non-judgement walk
Go to a busy place where you can walk around. It might be a shopping centre on a Saturday, or a busy city neighbourhood at rush hour. Practise mindful walking. Get pushed. Get cut off by cars. Hear people shout. Hear babies cry. See things you hate. See things you love. Discover things you crave. Notice whatever pops into your head. Can you see people without judging them? Can you see their actions as actions, without attaching any extra labels to them? When you notice judgements exploding in your head, can you bring your awareness back to the present moment? Can you enjoy being you?

2. The wrong opinions
Watch a news network that features shows and pundits that you disagree with vehemently. (You can also do this with a TV show you hate, or one that you often avoid because you think it's stupid or crass.) Sit in front of those shows. Notice how judgements emerge in your head. Can you hear people say things that are wrong, accept that they're wrong, but not let their words take control of your mood? Can you be you, while hearing and seeing things that are wrong? Instead of getting angry about fixing those wrong opinions, can you get excited about pouring yourself into building a community that's healthy for you and those around you?

3. The distracted worker
Do your work in a busy, noisy place. I especially like to do this exercise in chaotic food courts at a shopping centres or on public transport. I'll write something that I know I'll be sending to somebody or publishing online. That makes my brain worry about making a mistake because I'm not writing in the 'right' type of place.

Don't try to block out the noise with headphones. Notice how you judge the environment and your ability to work in it. Notice how you judge people that annoy you? Can you identify what you value in getting that work done? Can you align your actions with your values, recognising that controlling your environment and those around you is not something you're able to do? Can you bring your awareness back to your work when your thoughts start chasing after judgements about things happening in your environment?

EVERYTHING IN YOUR HEAD IS WEATHER

STEP 17

Make happiness a practice

'When I've felt things I want to brush off and deny as real, they always come back to haunt me and make me unhappy. To handle them, the first step I take is giving those feelings some space to exist. Then I try to express them in a real way, like writing them down, talking about them with someone I trust, or even taking a photo that helps me remember them. Even if taking a photo doesn't say exactly what I'm feeling in words, it becomes a mental bookmark for me to reference bad feelings – and make something in the process that connects with what I'm passionate about.'

Matt

As you learn to practise non-judgement and you're not constantly judging yourself and the world around you, you'll notice that you experience less of the feelings you don't like: less fear, anxiety, anger, frustration, envy, disappointment and so on. But the absence of fear is not the presence of happiness. As we've discussed, pursuing escape from those feelings as a goal will only lead to more of them. Happiness is its own distinct practice.

Earlier, when we talked about switching the fuel for your life from fear to values, I shared that story about walking out in the morning and panicking because I had nothing to be anxious about. One of the factors that made me so anxious was that I didn't know how to be happy without having fear or anxiety to control and then feeling happy about controlling them. For my entire life, I believed happiness meant controlling my fears. Fear and anxiety were necessary for my experience of happiness. I thought I could only be happy when I defeated my enemies.

If you believe that happiness only comes after defeating enemies, then you need to keep enemies in your life so you can keep on trying to defeat them. If you want more happiness, you need more enemies, or more challenging enemies. But any happiness you find after defeating a particular enemy will quickly fade and you'll need to find a new one to battle. If you take that approach with things like anxiety or stress or relationship problems, you'll always be bringing problems back into your life in search of happiness on the other side of them. More happiness will require increased levels of stress and anxiety and heartbreak. If you believe you'll only be happy when you're certain that people respect you, you'll require uncertainty about being disrespected. If you believe you can only be happy when you get rid of intrusive thoughts, you'll require intrusive thoughts, at ever increasing levels of severity. If you want to eliminate the urges to engage in your addictions so you can finally be happy, or do your work, or have a meaningful relationship, the cravings only become more and more severe because you've made the battle with them a prerequisite to living your life. That's the fear-fuelled approach to happiness. With that approach, you commit yourself to constant, never-ending war with the experiences you hate.

End the war.

You don't have to win it. You don't have to prove anything wrong. You don't have to make your fears go away. You don't have to be certain. Leave the uncertainties hanging there.

Walk off the battlefield.

Let the things you hate scream and shout at you. They can hang around and watch you build happiness. Their presence doesn't negate or contradict happiness unless you stop the practice of happiness and go off and fight them, leaving happiness neglected.

Walking off this battlefield is challenging. As much as you might hate fighting and struggling with the enemies inside you, you might not know of any other way to live. Your identity might have become dependent on your enemies.

YOU MIGHT HAVE STOCKHOLM SYNDROME

You've been kidnapped. Your kidnapper beats you and keeps you locked in a cage that he's forced you to help him build. He's threatened your family and your friends, he's taken you away from everything you've always dreamed about. He verbally harasses you and emotionally torments you. You don't dare try to venture out of your cage for fear of punishment. You're terrified that he could pop out from behind a corner at any moment. He's imprinted this fear into your gut so intensely that he doesn't even have to lock the tiny, cramped cage to which you've wilfully confined your life. You could leave, but what if he came back? What would he do to you? What if you started doing something you'd always wanted to do and then he showed up? What if it's worse than last time? And really it's not so bad being trapped here anyway. You don't have to worry about all sorts of things that bothered you in the past. They're out of your life now. And even though he beats you and ruins your life, he does give you pizza and ice cream. There are far fewer things to worry about when you live in a cage. Besides, the bars of your cage aren't actually trapping you, they're protecting you! There are worse catastrophes out there! You know because you've worried about them. You've imagined them in painstaking, bone-aching detail. Being in this cage is simply who you are. It's for the best. You're not like other people. And you're happy in the cage ... Well ... maybe 'happy' isn't the right word. You're mildly not panicked ... right now. That's like happiness, right?

One of the biggest challenges I see people encountering on the journey to build better mental health is that they develop Stockholm Syndrome with their compulsions. 'Stockholm Syndrome' is a term given to describe the experience of identifying with and even defending your kidnappers or abusers. On the one hand, you hate the experience of being trapped and anxious and not being able to live your life the way you want to. On the other hand, you really enjoy the brief moments of relief and certainty that come from trying to control your fears and avoid feelings you don't like.

You can complain for years about your struggles with anxiety, absolutely hate the compulsive behaviours that you engage in, feel so miserable about the opportunities you let slip by because you listened to the fears your brain threw at you, and still, when offered the chance to change, many, if not most people will turn down the opportunity to escape. The change looks too difficult, too uncertain, and they worry about losing the perceived benefits of their compulsions. They cease to recognise that they're in a prison. They start to believe the bars are actually protecting them, not trapping them. Their hatred for their symptoms is only trumped by their fear of actually escaping them.

Expect this to happen. After years of repeatedly pacing around this prison, your brain will not want to leave it. The kidnapper it knows causes less anxiety than the freedom it doesn't understand.

TRACK FUNCTIONING, NOT FEELINGS

You're going to walk off that battlefield, you're going to step out of that prison, and you're going to start doing the things you've always wanted to do. It's entirely possible it'll feel terrible.

When you're first making big changes in your life, you'll be riding up and down the Unhappiness Curve over and over again. You're innovating. As you're making the shift from a fear-fuelled, reactive life to one that's fuelled by your values, you'll struggle. You'll feel things you hate. You'll often feel like you're failing, that things will never get better, that you don't deserve to get better, that it's too challenging, that it's not working... Think all of that and more. Feel it all. Make space for it. With time and practice, you'll be able to welcome those experiences with gratitude and compassion. To start with, simply allowing them to be there without letting them throw you off course is enough. We can practise mindfulness with whatever we're feeling or thinking.

This might sound strange but the practice of happiness isn't about feeling happy right now. It's about doing the things that help you be happy and healthy over the long term. Happiness is a natural result of doing what you value. In the short term, aligning your actions with your values won't necessarily make you feel happy. When you accept uncertainty, anxiety and other feelings you don't like and align your actions with your values, instead of reacting with compulsions, you'll often feel terrible. It's stressful. Building great mental health and emotional fitness is messy, like improving physical fitness. You will doubt yourself. You will think you're failing. You will want to quit. You'll feel weak. You'll feel like you're not improving.

Don't leave this journey up to your brain's perception of what you're feeling and how you're progressing. Remember that sticky note: 'Are you sure of your perceptions?' Instead of relying on your brain's perceptions of your feelings, track your functioning.

Functioning is your ability to do what you want to do in life. Improving mental health is all about functioning – developing the capacity to feel whatever you're feeling while doing what matters to you in life. Track that capacity to do what matters to you. Are you continuing to cut out compulsions listed on your Hierarchy (page 84)? Are you consistently doing the activities on your Awesome Schedule (page 108)? Are you practising non-judgement? Are you accepting whatever uncertainties that monster in your head throws at you? Are you sticking to your values with each step you take?

The practice of being yourself, even when it leads to experiences you don't like, can still be a practice full of happiness. You may discover, however, that you're not as skilled at feeling happiness as you are at feeling things such as anxiety and fear. To help yourself stay outside the cage or off the battlefield, we need to work on developing your capacity to experience feelings you like.

HAPPINESS IS TOUGH

It's tough to feel happy. Hating people is easy. Trying to avoid pain is easy. Trying to control uncertainty is easy. These are all practices that make us miserable and hurt us, but they're easier than feeling happiness and risking its loss. It's easier to say that I'm trapped in a cage right now so I can't do the things I want to do in life. It's easier to react to the fear of an enemy than it is to step off the battlefield into the uncertainty and freedom of creating your life.

In Step 7 on coping with compulsions, we talked about accepting feelings we don't like, but are you also willing to accept happiness? Or love? Developing your emotional fitness isn't only about learning how to handle feelings you don't like. Accepting feelings like love and happiness will help you do more of what makes you happy. It will help you deepen your relationships. It will help you prevent yourself from dropping back into the familiar comfort of constantly trying to solve the feelings you hate.

Feelings like love and happiness are also experiences we try to control because we're unsure how to handle them. We stick extra meanings on to them. We become afraid of losing what we've always wanted. We get caught in IF X THEN Y loops. We push people away because we don't want to get hurt, or we don't want to hurt them.

Are you skilled at feeling anxious? Do you have great capacity when it comes to hating? Can you spend a day being upset about a comment a stranger made online? Can you spend an entire week being anxious about a project at work, from the moment you wake up each day until you knock yourself out with sleeping pills at night? Can you spend a month hating your ex-boyfriend, constantly obsessing about him, time-travelling into the past to argue with him?

These are incredible skills that require impressive endurance. It speaks to the years of practice we invest in feeling anxiety and hatred that we can hold these emotions for such long periods of time.

We can do the same with emotions like happiness, love or compassion. But they require a similar amount of practice. In the same way that we practise compulsions to give ourselves more of the emotions we don't like, we can practise skills such as mindfulness, we can embrace uncertainty, and we can do things we value to experience more of the feelings we do enjoy. One of the ways we can improve our ability to experience happiness is through the practice of gratitude.

YOU CAN EXPRESS GRATITUDE IN ANY MOMENT

What I find most effective is bringing the practice of gratitude into my daily life with the simplest of activities. It's not about adding up the 'good' things that happened and feeling grateful for them. It's about feeling grateful for what I'm doing right now. If I'm making myself a sandwich, I can be grateful for nourishing myself. When I'm sitting and breathing, I can be grateful for my lungs. They do so much work for me and I don't even ask them to do it! I can be grateful for the floor beneath me. It's holding me up! I can be grateful for the ability to read and write. How else could I find the word 'chocolate' so quickly on the dessert menu? I can be grateful for all of the people that worked to build the place in which I live. Maybe those people are all dead now but I can experience their hard work. I can feel gratitude towards the people I walk past on the street. It's much more enjoyable to feel gratitude instead of fear or hatred or disgust or envy. Those people don't need to do anything specific for me. Feeling gratitude towards somebody is an enjoyable experience without requiring a reason to do it.

When I'm getting ready to leave the house in the morning, I can feed myself, wash myself, brush my teeth, clip my nose hairs, clean my ears, put on clothes, and do whatever else I might do, all as practices of gratitude and appreciation to myself. I could also do all of that out of fear of what I think others will think about me, or maybe out of fear for my health or my career. It all depends on what skills I want to practise and what I want my brain to think about during the day.

If you spend a significant amount of time getting ready in the morning, doing your hair, putting on make-up or coordinating the perfect outfit, that practice can become an opportunity to feel gratitude towards yourself. If you spend that time each morning appreciating your body, you'll discover that has many benefits throughout your life. If you spend that time each morning trying to control your body or appearance in the hopes of controlling what others think about you, that's a serious amount of time invested in fear and anxiety that will also have very natural results (which you won't like).

You don't need to find more time in your life to feel gratitude towards yourself. You can take advantage of what you're already doing simply by changing your intentions. Again, this is about making the switch from fear-fuelled actions to value-fuelled actions:

- Instead of brushing your teeth because you want to avoid bad breath or make sure there isn't a piece of spinach stuck there, try brushing your teeth as appreciation for all of the hard chewing those teeth have done for you.
- Instead of putting on your clothes while obsessing about what you think those clothes will make others think about you, try putting on your clothes as a way of expressing yourself, or keeping yourself warm or comfortable. It's also an opportunity to feel gratitude to all of the people who worked to make those clothes. It's very likely that somebody on the other side of the world stitched together the clothes you're wearing, in a workplace that you couldn't imagine working in, for an amount of money that you can't imagine living on. You are connected to a global network of people that make your life possible.

- Instead of eating to control your body, or punish it, or chase away feelings, try eating to fuel the practice of being you. You're giving energy to each cell in your body. Offer that food in gratitude to all of the organs inside you that work tirelessly day and night to keep you working. Feel gratitude for all of the people that worked to bring that food from the fields to your stomach. If you're eating an animal, don't ignore that. It was alive once, like you. You can appreciate what it means to be alive.

There are so many opportunities to practise gratitude in your daily life, doing the things you're already doing. Explore why you do what you do. What do you want your brain to think about? Are you starting off your day with an hour or two of meditation on anxiety, or on gratitude? That's your practice. Practise whatever skill at which you hope to become adept.

I understand how difficult it can be to even imagine thinking positively about yourself, let alone expressing feelings of gratitude towards yourself or others on a regular basis. The exercise for this step is a very old and popular practice that will help you develop the capacity to feel and express emotions like gratitude, compassion, kindness and love.

EXERCISE: Loving Kindness Meditation

I typically take my meditation the same way I take my green tea: with no extra things in it. But I do make some exceptions with my meditation practice (although never with tea), and loving kindness, or *metta,* meditation is one such exception.

Loving kindness meditation is a practice that got me into the idea of emotional fitness because I found it so physically difficult to feel emotions such as love and kindness and gratitude, particularly towards myself. As with any exercise, that difficulty is a helpful sign of something that needs practising.

I'll include a written guide here that you can read through, but I encourage you to seek out audio guides you can follow. Try different styles, work with experienced teachers in person – whatever helps you build up your skills with this practice. This is a valuable practice for building your capacity to feel emotions you might not practise nearly as much as you practise emotions you hate. You can't expect your brain to be skilled at feeling love and kindness without a serious amount of practice.

1. Grab a seat and get comfortable.
2. Close your eyes and breathe normally. Notice where you're in contact with the floor or the seat beneath you. Be with that awareness for several breaths.
3. Then slowly bring your awareness up your body. Take a couple of breaths at each body part. Say hello to each one. Notice the posture of your body. And bring your awareness up your torso to your chest.
4. Be aware of yourself breathing in. Be aware of yourself breathing out.
5. Spend some time meditating like this, slowing down your thoughts, getting your brain to sit with you as you breathe. Notice whatever you're feeling and welcome that. You might be anxious. You might want to think about problems at work or school or in a relationship. That's all OK. When your thoughts start to run off again, gently bring your awareness back to your breath. Notice how your body moves with each inhale and each exhale.
6. When you're ready, bring to mind something that makes you feel happy and warm and loving. It might be a person, an animal, a particular event, a place, etc. My teacher/instructor Ronit sometimes calls this a 'warm-hearted' feeling. Picture that thing or that experience. Notice how it makes you feel. Be aware

of the physical experience of that thing you love. Breathe into that feeling and let it extend to every part of your body.
7. If you notice your awareness has wandered off to worry about whether you've received any responses to your online dating profile or whether that pain in your gut is cancer, simply return to the thing that gives you that warm-hearted feeling and breathe that feeling back into your body.
8. Towards whatever you brought to mind to give you that warm-hearted feeling, express that feeling back towards it in gratitude. Feel that loving kindness flow from you, into it.
9. If you want to express that feeling of loving kindness in words, go for it. Wish them health, and happiness, and freedom. But continue to feel that expression of emotion at a level deeper than words.
10. Repeat steps 8 and 9, and each time bring to mind a different person to express loving kindness towards. Here's a suggestion on how you might structure this:

- Begin with somebody you care for deeply, somebody you would be happy to see.
- Then move on to an acquaintance that you have no particular feelings about. Enjoy feeling loving kindness towards somebody who owes you nothing and to whom you owe nothing.
- Then bring to mind somebody that you hate. It could be somebody who's hurt you or hurt people around you. Notice the judgements and thoughts that arise around that person. You don't have to argue with them or prove them wrong. Feeling loving kindness towards them does not change or contradict anything they've done to you or anybody else. Can you express love and kindness towards somebody who's

caused pain to you or those you care about? This isn't supposed to be easy. Push into it as if you're weightlifting. Can you feel compassion for a person because they're a person?
- Then try feeling loving kindness to yourself. This might be even more difficult than loving somebody who's hurt you. Can you look past your judgements of yourself and embrace you for being you? Can you wish health, happiness and freedom to yourself?
- To finish, you could bring to mind a group of people, such as your community, some people you know are struggling or perhaps the entire world. Spread that feeling of loving kindness to all of them. Enjoy that connection with so many people.
- If at any point you feel your warm-hearted batteries depleting, return to that initial thing that helped you bring up that feeling.
- Take as much time as you need with this. There's no need to rush through. Enjoy the practice!

PRACTISE GRATITUDE WITH THE SAME DEDICATION YOU PRACTISED FEAR

STEP 18

Embrace uncertainty

> 'The main challenge for me in recovery from OCD was trusting that the obsessions and fears weren't true. I only turned the corner towards recovery when I surrendered to the idea that I may never know, and only then did OCD loosen its grip. The only thing that is certain is uncertainty, and that's OK!'
>
> Stuart

We're constantly encountering new uncertainties around us, or dragging old ones along with us from the past, or inventing new ones about the future all on our own. If you hold on to beliefs about uncertainty being a very bad thing or being something that needs resolving, then practising happiness can become very difficult because doing things you value will require you to leave many uncertainties unresolved. Even if you don't engage in compulsions to resolve uncertainties, you'll still experience uncertainty constantly. That can be a very unpleasant and stressful experience, or it can become an experience that helps you thrive. In this step we'll unpack some of the uncertainty baggage you might be carrying around with you and we'll look at how pushing into uncertainty is the path forward to being yourself.

SEEKING OUT UNCERTAINTY

This goes all the way back to that very first exercise we did to practise not checking our phones (page 13). I emphasised then the importance of learning to tackle easier uncertainties so you could develop the capacity to handle the ones that actually bothered you. Now, with everything you've learned, consider how you can take that simple exercise and turn it into a lifestyle that supports doing what you value.

You don't even have to wait for uncertainties to pop up. You can seek them out. You can find opportunities to expose yourself to uncertainty.

When you get the urge to Google the guy you're about to go out with on a date, can you sit with that uncertainty and then make a decision about whether it's a useful way to invest your time? Can you take on a new task at work that's unfamiliar and admit that you don't know what you're doing? Can you sit in that uncertainty and learn new skills? Can you take on a challenge when you don't know if you'll fail or succeed? Maybe you can't lift that weight, or you won't pass the test, or there won't be anybody there you know, or you will be responsible for things going wrong. Can you accept those uncertainties and still be yourself while you take steps forward? Can you focus on enjoying the steps you're taking instead of getting caught up in chasing an outcome far off in the future that may or may not even be real?

When you start to take this broad approach to embracing uncertainty, every moment of the day becomes an opportunity to care for your mental health and develop your capacity to handle experiences you avoided in the past. Every time you find an uncertainty to embrace, you free up a little bit more of your time and energy to spend on things that actually matter to you.

SO DO I HAVE TO SPEND THE REST OF MY LIFE DOING THINGS THAT MAKE ME ANXIOUS?

Imagine a kid named Simon who goes to the zoo with his school class. Simon really wants to go and see the chameleons. He's a huge fan of chameleons. He knows everything there is to know about them. They have cells called chromatophores that help them change colour, and their eyes can look in two directions at once, and their tongues can be twice the length of their bodies. They are *amazing*. His mother won't let him have one so he's super excited to see live chameleons at the zoo today.

But when he gets off the bus with the other students, the big popular school bully slaps him on the back of the head and says, 'Hey, new guy, come and check out the rhinos with us.'

Simon is new to this school and he doesn't have many friends. He's afraid that if he doesn't go with the popular kids, they'll be mean to him in the future, so he goes along with them to see the rhinos, even though he thinks rhinos are boring. He's worried about having time to see the chameleons. The reptile house is on the other side of the zoo from the rhinos.

The boys throw some rocks at the rhinos and try to scare them but the rhinos don't do anything. One of the boys suggests they go and see the tigers next door. Simon thinks about excusing himself from the group but that only makes him anxious. Would they think he doesn't like them? Would they be mean to him later? How would he even tell the group he was leaving without it being really awkward? What if they think chameleons are lame? He decides to stay. He'll try to be like a chameleon and blend in with the group. He can make the same jokes about the girls. He can say cool things and be cool so people think he's cool.

Simon is very small and he's always afraid that other boys won't think he's tough. When he sees the tigers sleeping in their pen, he says, 'I thought they would look scarier. They look like house cats.' He thinks that's a very tough thing to say. People will think he's tough now. But what actually happens is that the bully says, 'I dare you to touch one. Just run in, touch it and run back.' And then two of the other boys grab Simon, easily lift him up, and toss him over the fence into the tiger enclosure.

Simon has never been so afraid in his life. A tiger opens its eyes and snarls at him. His heart is racing. He's so panicked that his head feels like it's about to explode. He doesn't know what to do. He doesn't know what's going to happen. But he's heard that reacting to anxiety and uncertainty is a compulsion. He's very anxious right now and incredibly uncertain about whether he'll get mauled by a tiger. So does that mean he needs to touch the tiger? That he should push into this uncertainty? Is it a compulsion to avoid his fear? Isn't he supposed to turn towards difficult emotions?

The tiger eats Simon.

If we look at the big picture of what happened that day, there was a series of compulsions that led to Simon being in that tiger's stomach: reacting to the uncertainty about being liked, trying to control what others thought about him, not being honest, etc. Whether it's a compulsion or not to avoid touching the tiger is irrelevant. By consistently controlling and avoiding uncertainty about what might happen if he went and did what he wanted to do, he very naturally ended up in a situation that created even more uncertainty and fear.

Improving emotional fitness and learning how to handle internal and external experiences is something we do in service of and aligned with our values. We're not doing this for the sake of doing it. We're doing it to live our lives.

PICK YOUR (CREATIVE) BATTLES

You can draw a line from where you are to where you want to be, like a path through uncharted wilderness, and that path will take you through an astounding number of uncertainties. That path will also be surrounded by uncertainties on all sides calling for your attention. Embracing uncertainty is as much about charging headfirst into the uncertainties that obscure the path ahead as it is about walking past the uncertainties that lie to the side of your path. There's nothing wrong with uncertainty. You don't have to solve uncertainties simply because they exist. If you step off the path to chase after them, you'll never get to where you want to be and you'll spend the rest of your life digging around in the undergrowth for certainty about things you don't even care about.

In the past, if I read something in an article that I didn't know about, I'd immediately look it up, and then I'd discover something in that article I didn't know about so I'd dig up a documentary on that and spend two hours watching it out of the corner of my eye while sitting on the sofa, checking my messages on my phone, reading the news and looking up more things I didn't know about. I was like a raccoon trying to catch the water spraying out of a lawn sprinkler. The flow of uncertainties didn't stop and I didn't stop trying to resolve them.

But when I experience uncertainties like those, I need to reflect on whether reacting to them will help me do something I value or if this is simply my brain trying to chase certainty like a dog that runs after every stick. I liked spending my time chasing after every little thing that interested me. I hated that I never accomplished any of the things that I actually wanted to do.

This isn't about stifling creativity, curiosity or exploration. This is about being able to choose the uncertainties you do explore. It's about what's useful for creating and building.

If you're about to get into an argument with your partner because you want to correct something they said, ask yourself how resolving that will help you create the relationship you want to have with your partner. If you're about to embark on learning a new skill, ask yourself if that's going to help you do the types of things that help you find meaning in life. If you're about to do an exposure exercise because you want to get over a fear, ask yourself if you're doing this to experience more in life or if you're doing it because you're afraid of fear and want to avoid it.

BUT WHAT IF I'M UNCERTAIN ABOUT THE PAST?

We've mostly been exploring uncertainty in the present, but many of the uncertainties you might be troubled by or trying to resolve could be from the past. What if I hurt her? Why did they hurt me? What really happened that night? Why did I fail? What if everybody finds out what I've done? Will that mistake come back to haunt me?

They're like these big bags of rubbish you drag around because you're looking for the right place and the right way to dispose of them. When you do that, those uncertainties from the past very much become part of the present because of how they limit what you can do and where you can go.

It's OK to be uncertain about the past. If you believe you need to resolve the past before you can move on, or you believe you need to be certain about the past – that you need to dispose of this rubbish in the 'right' way – you'll take yourself far away from your path in the hope of finding the mythical incinerators of closure and resolution.

Rubbish happens. When your brain reminds you of that, you can judge those experiences, feel terrible about them and engage in compulsions in pursuit of changing them, just like with any experience. All of the same skills we've discussed about handling uncertainty apply to the past, the present and the future. That doesn't mean avoiding feelings or pretending things didn't happen. Bring compassion and love to those memories to work on loosening your grip on those bags of rubbish so you can just drop them where they are. They don't have to influence each new step you take. We'll explore a popular, albeit challenging exercise for doing that next.

EXERCISE: Healing the Inner Child

These bags of rubbish we carry around with us typically get handed to us when we're young. Maybe somebody you loved told you that you were worthless. They handed you a bag with a little memory of worthlessness rotting inside it. Carrying around that rubbish everywhere started to affect what you did and how you did it. That led to you collecting more pieces of worthlessness. The bag got heavier. It interfered in your life more and more. You picked up other bags of rubbish. Now you might have some very large bags full of rubbish memories. This meditation practice is about starting the process of emptying those bags.

We'll build on the Loving Kindness Meditation from the previous step. Healing the inner child is a way that you can apply that skill of bringing loving kindness to difficult emotions and experiences.

1. Grab a seat and get comfortable.
2. Close your eyes and breathe normally. Notice where you're in contact with the floor or the seat beneath you. Be with that awareness of touch for several breaths.
3. Then bring your awareness up your body. Notice your posture. Notice your chest moving in and out as you breathe.
4. Spend some time meditating like this, slowing down your mind, getting it to sit with you. Notice whatever you're feeling and welcome that. You might be anxious about what's coming up. That's OK. Gently bring your awareness back to your breath. Notice each inhale. Follow each exhale until it ends. Smile into the brief pause before you inhale again.
5. Take a moment to appreciate your body. Think of something very normal that it's done lately, like helping you carry groceries. Feel gratitude to your body for that. Bring up that feeling of love and kindness you practised with Loving Kindness Meditation. Feel that in appreciation of a particular part of your

body, or maybe your breath, for keeping you running and living without you even needing to tell it to do anything.
6. Soak in that appreciation for several breaths. Feel it as if it was a gift you were holding. Rest that gift in your lap.
7. Now you'll go back to that time in the past when you felt the pain that's become part of that knot inside you. It might be an embarrassing situation at school, a time you were scared, a decision you regret, a day you wish you could forget, a moment when somebody you hate said hurtful things to you that you still repeat in your head. Picture the place where the painful event happened. Hear the sounds, smell it, remember what it looked like. Picture any other people that were there.
8. This exercise is partly to practise cognitive defusion. See your current self in that place as well, watching the experience unfold. See your younger self as separate from you. You're going back to this painful place as you are now, knowing what you know now. You're going back to help that younger version of you. Picture both of your selves there.
9. Remember what that experience felt like for that younger version of you. What did that younger version of yourself feel at that time? What was racing through your head? What would you say to that younger you? What would you want yourself to know? How can you help that person? How can you bring other people together to help them? What can you share from your more recent experiences?
10. Give that younger you that gift of gratitude and love and kindness you have with you. Feel yourself expressing it to your younger self. That younger you took on such a big challenge and so much suffering.

You know how frightening that was. Extend kindness to that person. You understand why that person still carries this pain. Stay there with that feeling as long as you like. Help them.

11. When you feel like it, hug that younger version of yourself. Encompass them in love and compassion as if you're wrapping a bandage around them to help heal the pain. When you feel ready, absorb them inside you with love. That younger you is still with you. Sit with that awareness of how you got to where you are. Breathe into who you are now.

12. When you're ready, bring your awareness back to your body. Notice your breath, notice how you're in contact with the floor or the seat beneath you. Take some time to breathe. Breathe into that awareness of yourself being in a complex world moving around you. Slowly open your eyes and bring yourself back into contact with your surroundings.

13. It will take some time to help that younger version of yourself. You may revisit that particular place several times as you slowly work out this experience. You might uncover other places and experiences you want to practise on as you loosen that knot.

Something to keep in mind as you explore this practice: you might cry. That's OK. You might get very angry. That's OK. Whatever feelings arise are totally OK. There might be many uncomfortable things blocked up behind that knot. It might be very difficult to no longer be fearful and humiliated by that experience. These experiences are often ones around which we develop Stockholm Syndrome. We can't imagine not being afraid of them. We can't imagine that we're deserving of compassion and love. We can't imagine moving on from them. We can't imagine not feeling guilt about them. But all of that is possible.

230   The Transformation

STEP 19

Plan for your wilderness adventure

'I cut out most of my compulsions and began trying to do things proactively instead of reactively, but I still felt very anxious all the time. I realized that acting on my values was something I was doing to try to get rid of anxiety. Letting go of my constant focus on my emotions was the final key to letting go of my remaining anxiety.'

Kamran

With each step we take in life, we're moving forward through a fantastic wilderness obstacle course. All of the work we've been doing throughout this book is to help improve our mental health and emotional fitness so we can handle any obstacle and keep moving through this wilderness towards our values. On this adventure, we'll swim across lakes, scale cliffs, admire the beautiful view, hack our way through the undergrowth, prance through meadows, wrestle beasts that get in our way, and achieve the unthinkable. This is not going to be an easy hike, so in this step we'll explore the five most common barriers I see people running into as they apply the skills we've discussed. Those five barriers are:

1. Believing you're a unique and special snowflake.
2. Trying to get understanding.
3. Not dismantling the systems in your life built around your compulsions.
4. Mistaking environmental changes for changes in skill or ability.
5. Wanting to avoid relapse.

That fifth one might sound odd but, paradoxically, I think it's the most important barrier to overcome if you're going to avoid relapsing back into the pain, stress and compulsions that were getting in the way of life. Let's tackle these barriers.

BARRIER 1: BELIEVING YOU'RE A UNIQUE AND SPECIAL SNOWFLAKE

Working with people from all over the world on their mental health, I cannot emphasise enough how similar we all are in the mental health challenges we encounter every day, in every culture, across all genders, across socioeconomic classes, in every imaginable environment. Whatever it is you've been dealing with, I guarantee somebody in Port Moresby, Papua New Guinea, is dealing with the exact same thing right this very minute.

It's also true that we're running through this obstacle course each with our own set of experiences, privileges and resources. That can lead to this barrier of believing we're unique coming up in a couple of ways. For instance, your resources may help you overcome some challenges easily. That might make you think you don't need to take care of your mental health like other people, that once you've cut out the compulsions getting in your way, you don't need to deal with the others. You can manage them! You're more capable than other people! But all you've done there is to mistake your resources and privileges for your abilities. If those get removed for some reason, you'll find yourself struggling.

The opposite can also happen: you find yourself struggling to utilise a support – something like meditation – or you run into a challenge that seems more difficult for you than it does for somebody else. That doesn't necessarily mean there's something unique about your brain that disqualifies you from making use of that support or overcoming that challenge. What we need to look at are things we can change around you that will help you to keep moving forward.

Expect your brain to invent reasons why the adventure ahead is too difficult for you. Also expect it to come up with very convincing arguments as to why you don't need to prepare for the challenges ahead in the same way that other people do. Don't listen to those reasons or you'll end up going nowhere.

BARRIER 2: TRYING TO GET UNDERSTANDING

You may want to explain to co-workers why you've taken some time off, or you want society to be more accepting and understanding of mental health issues, or you may want your family to understand how they're making healthy changes more difficult for you. This is all understandable, but it'll still become a barrier because trying to control what other people think is a compulsion. If you try to get understanding from other people you'll consistently be disappointed, and whatever feeling it was you hoped to get from their understanding will continue to elude you. People can't give you a feeling that only comes from within you. Instead of trying to get understanding, give it – and that's going to happen in the form of communication about where you're going.

Imagine you're a driver in a busy city that has no traffic lights. Lisbon in Portugal has many intersections without traffic lights or stop signs. I was once on the edge of the large park, the Jardim do Principe Real, in an older part of the city, and as I crossed the street at a busy intersection, a car turned right, a car came straight through the intersection, and a car turned left, all at the exact same time. All three cars were aiming for the same single lane of the street that myself and several other pedestrians were crossing at that moment. Everybody had to communicate what they were doing. Everybody crossed safely. No one person in that situation could expect anybody else to understand what they were doing or where they wanted to go. What was important was that everybody made clear what they needed to get to where they needed to be.

Life doesn't have traffic lights or stop signs so we need to communicate. Give understanding to where other people are going. Communicate where you're going to those who will play a role in helping you get there.

BARRIER 3: NOT DISMANTLING THE SYSTEMS IN YOUR LIFE BUILT AROUND YOUR COMPULSIONS

One of the biggest challenges we can encounter to improving our mental health can be the people with whom we've developed relationships through our compulsions. As you're trying to cut out those compulsions and do things you value, those people will be trying to push you back into your compulsions, sometimes intentionally, sometimes accidentally.

For example, if you were a manager and you engaged in many compulsions micromanaging your staff, you'd probably build systems in your office that encouraged those compulsions and forced people to work in unhealthy ways. Your staff would get accustomed to that. Their incentives, financial or social, would be aligned with that old way of working. So when you start to change things, they're going to encounter uncertainty and they'll react to that by falling back on what they've done before.

As you make healthy changes, you need either to bring other people with you, or recognise that you may no longer be moving forward together. This gets especially complex when you're dealing with romantic or family relationships. We're social animals and losing relationships scares us. If we build relationships around our compulsions but then remove the compulsions, we need to decide if there's a way to build those relationships around things we actually want to keep in our lives.

If you're running into challenges with other people, try doing the Compulsion Journey exercise (page 98) with a focus on interpersonal relationships, to make these systems visible and find opportunities for change.

BARRIER 4: MISTAKING ENVIRONMENTAL CHANGES FOR CHANGES IN ABILITY

Terrain changes. That's a natural part of any journey, whether you're progressing or regressing. Different terrain will require different skills. In a swampy area, you might hop from one log to the next. In a steep area you'll climb with all your limbs and be drenched in sweat when you reach the top. Across a flat meadow you can walk easily.

If you struggled with social anxieties and decided to avoid people by never leaving your house, you'd probably experience a reduction in anxiety (for a short period of time). But that doesn't mean you've learned how to handle your social anxiety issues or that they've gone away. Walking in a circle around a meadow does not mean you know how to climb a mountain.

Conversely, somebody who is progressing along smoothly may encounter an especially difficult environment. That doesn't mean they've developed an illness or lost their abilities. It's very normal initially to fail at something that's new and difficult. Experience that difficulty. It doesn't necessarily mean you've regressed. It might mean you're moving forward and, as part of that, you've encountered a new environment. Understand that environment and the skills you need to develop so you can navigate it effectively.

BARRIER 5: WANTING TO AVOID RELAPSE

When I talk about relapse here, I mean the return of thoughts, feelings, or compulsions that you want to get out of your life. It could be that depression kept you from engaging with your family the way that you would like, so you don't want that to happen anymore. Or you had a panic attack once in class and you don't want to have that experience again. Or you struggled with intrusive thoughts that made you question everything in life. That terrified you and you don't want to go back to living with those thoughts and images in your head. Whatever it was, you don't want it to happen again. That's understandable. When our mental health isn't in great shape, it's a traumatising experience.

That's why we do the work we've covered in this book: we learn to experience the stuff in our heads, we cut out compulsions, we make changes in the systems around us, we practise doing the things we value. That all requires a lot of sweaty work, just like improving our physical fitness or making any other type of complex change.

As people are doing that work, I get asked a lot of questions, such as: 'If I cut out these compulsions and start doing more of what matters to me, I won't have this anxiety anymore, right?' But here's what's problematic about a question like that: it takes you back into compulsions.

Remember that a compulsion is anything you do to cope with, check on, or control uncertainty, anxiety and other feelings you don't like. You probably don't want to experience relapse because it will create uncertainty, cause you anxiety and sink you deep into all sorts of feelings you don't like. But that fear of falling back into those experiences is like any other fear or uncertainty. The moment you start reacting to it and putting it in charge of your life, you've already relapsed, even if you don't feel it yet.

If you truly want to get over a struggle with something like anxiety, stop wanting to avoid it. As long as you're chasing that desire, you're choosing to trap yourself in that experience you hate. This goes back to what we discussed about goals and changing desires. Trying to avoid experiences got you into this struggle. It will not get you out of it. So how do we get out of this trap? Through your actions.

Instead of wanting to avoid relapse, act in a way that builds better mental health. The best defence here is a steadfast, values-based attack in the form of mindful action, with each step you take. You don't have to worry about relapse because you have the skills now to handle whatever comes your way. You know how to tame monsters. You can even ride them places you never believed were accessible to you. You can experience any disturbing thought and you know how to accept it, not judge it and not conflate it with your identity. You can recognise when you're engaging in compulsions and, instead of judging yourself, you can choose to do something you value. You can create and build and proactively do the things that make you happy and healthy over the long term.

You know how to practise being yourself while experiencing things you don't like. Keep practising.

ONE MORE EXERCISE

In the final step, I haven't included an exercise. That's because once you have finished reading the book, the only exercise is to continually develop your own personal mental health and fitness lifestyle around the skills and concepts we've explored. But there is one more exercise I want to share with you. It combines so much of what you've learned, it'll help you overcome the barriers we have just discussed, and it's an exercise you can apply in your life every day. The understanding that comes from this simple exercise has helped me maintain my mental health, continued to improve it and kept my steps through the wilderness of life moving in a direction that matters to me.

EXERCISE: What's On Your Path?

Since you're about to apply all of your new emotional fitness skills on this adventure through the wilderness, it'll help to have a map. We don't know exactly what the terrain will be like, however, so this is a map that helps you understand where you are based on the mental and physical actions you engage in at any moment. Those actions are your steps. You can know whether you're wandering off the path based on the steps you're taking.

You hopefully have a clear understanding now of the actions that indicate you're way off the path and stuck, waist-deep, in a bog. And you understand what you value and how your values translate into actions. Those are the steps that are clearly on the path. The value of the exercise we're going to do now is in articulating the actions that are just off your path. Those are the seemingly 'normal' compulsions that might not bother you, but as you've seen, they're indicators you're beginning to head off in the wrong direction. By understanding the actions that are just a few steps off the path, you can empower yourself to spot problems sooner and correct course quickly. This is all part of being proactive and taking a values-based approach to our journey. We don't have to wait until we're lost to understand the value of sticking to what matters to us.

1. Divide a piece of paper into three columns. Label the columns: 'ON THE PATH', 'JUST OFF THE PATH', AND 'WAY OFF THE PATH'.
2. List the actions that go in each column. What are you going to do each day to be healthy and happy and work towards your goals in life? List all of that in the ON THE PATH column. What are the things you do that you consider totally misaligned with who you are and where you want to be in life? Put all of that under WAY

OFF THE PATH. What are the actions that set you up for or contribute to going off the path? That's what goes under the JUST OFF THE PATH column.
3. You'll probably work on this list several times as you learn more about what sinks you into unhealthy behaviours.
4. Be as specific as you can about the actions you list. For example, instead of writing something like 'Not avoiding triggers', you can consider what the triggers are and list the actions that will take you directly into them, like: 'Articulating my opinions in meetings', or 'Getting changed in front of others in the locker room', or 'Babysitting my friends' kids'.

Note that the actions in each column don't necessarily need to correlate across the columns. You might see some direct connections but that's not always the case. These actions are indicators, like sensors in your life telling you where you are. I'll share an example of some actions I would put in those three columns and you'll see what I mean:

ON THE PATH
- Volunteering.
- Going to the gym 5 times per week and consistently challenging myself to learn new skills, lift more, or go further.
- Cooking 90% of my own meals.
- Using social media to help people.
- Creating work I care about and sharing it publicly.

JUST OFF THE PATH
- Procrastinating on laundry, taking out the rubbish, or cleaning.
- Investing hours and hours in obsessing over relationships and hunting for dates.
- Buying breakfasts at restaurants (because I didn't get food shopping or take time to make my breakfast the night before).

WAY OFF THE PATH
- Checking doors, windows, locks, taps, appliances, etc.
- Lying to people.
- Getting into a relationship to escape loneliness.
- Missing out on sleep because I stayed up all night online.
- Not using knives.
- Reacting to fears of being poisoned, watched, or attacked.

ON THE PATH	JUST OFF THE PATH	WAY OFF THE PATH
• Collaborating with others and not working alone.	• Staying up late on my phone in bed.	• Always waiting for friends to contact me first.
• Sharing my meditation practice with others.	• Flipping through social media mindlessly.	• Asking for reassurance from my friends and family.
• Hosting friends at my home and feeding them.	• Making excuses to not meditate.	• Researching illness symptoms online.
• Intentionally spending time with family for no particular reason.	• Not tracking my budget.	• Quitting jobs, changing careers, and changing home every year or two.
• Going to a new place or doing something new in my city at least once per month.	• Refreshing my blog or email account to check for responses to posts or messages.	• Paying bills or taxes late.
• Setting aside time each month to experience nature and care for it.	• Spending hours watching series I don't like.	• Not showering or shaving.
	• Eating all of the chocolate in my cupboards.	• Buying expensive appliances I don't need and don't use.
	• Weighing myself.	

STEP 20

Keep taking steps

'I was afraid to speak publicly about my mental health challenges, but once I did, I was surprised to learn that a couple of friends were going through something similar. I was so relieved that I wasn't alone and we could now have conversations about this important aspect of our lives.'

Annie

You now have at your disposal the knowledge to help you build your own mental health and emotional fitness practice. You **understand that you are not a rock**, you're a human, so you feel things and think things. Sometimes you won't like those things, sometimes you'll love them, but when you're struggling, you won't get caught chasing after them. Instead, you'll **recognise your problems** and go after those, even when that requires complex changes in your life or the environment around you. As you work on those changes, you'll **practise mindfulness** and you'll **meditate** so you can build the capacity to experience whatever you're experiencing as you **follow your values**. That'll require you to **focus on changing actions, not thoughts or feelings**. No longer trying to change thoughts or feelings will mean you can stop compulsions. You'll **stop coping** and you'll **break your** IF X THEN Y **thinking pattern** so you can free yourself from the equations that keep you trapped in anxiety and stress. You'll **stop checking** and **you'll understand your fears** by digging into the reasons behind your compulsions, so you can uncover the issues you actually need to practise accepting. You'll **stop controlling** other people, your internal experiences, the past and the future. That'll be possible because you'll **tame the monster** of urges and fears in your head that throws uncertainties at you to trick you into feeding it compulsions. This will all lead to a major transformation in your life as you **switch your life's fuel from fear to values**. But don't go looking for motivation to make the switch. So you'll need to **break your motivation addiction**. Chasing that feeling is like chasing any other feeling. You might believe that motivation is necessary but that'll be just one of the beliefs you end up ditching. To succeed at sticking to your values you'll need to **throw out unhelpful beliefs and desires**. And you'll have the opportunity to rewrite your beliefs and desires every time you accept an experience, **practise non-judgement** and choose actions aligned with your values. You can show your brain your beliefs through your actions as you **make happiness a practice**, recognising that it's a skill, it comes only after regular, often challenging practise. Doing those things that actually make you happy, the things that matter to you in life, will require you to **embrace uncertainty** to an extent you probably never have before. That's part of innovating and exploring new territory. You're venturing into uncharted wilderness in your life so **plan for your wilderness adventure**. Support the work of living by your values as you combine all of these skills into the present moment and **keep taking steps** in the direction of your values.

The practice of accepting the stuff in your head and doing things you value is a practice you can enjoy every day for the rest of your life. There will be days when you struggle with that practice. There will be bad days, and terrible days, and absolutely horrible days. Make space for them. Feel them. You can trust yourself to experience them. In the present moment – the only place you can possibly be – you can always make a choice about how you act. As you become more skilled at making choices, you'll see that acting according to your values isn't only about yourself. It's about your community.

GO BEYOND YOU

There are many misconceptions about mindfulness and meditation, one of those being that they're solitary, self-focused practices, above the world and its troubles; things you do while hiding away in a hut up on a mountain cultivating pristine balance. But hopefully you've seen that these practices aren't about avoiding the world or feelings you don't like. These practices are about diving head-first into those experiences and swimming around in them to support long-term health and happiness. The fact is, your health is connected to your environment and the communities of people with which you interact, virtually and in the real world. Because of those multifaceted connections, you cannot build health and happiness without working on them at the community level – even the global level – alongside and connected to the changes you'll work on as an individual. Your health, comprising your physical and mental health, is not separate from your neighbours' health, the health of your public institutions, the health of the water systems you depend upon or the financial health of the young woman who picked the tomato you ate in your salad for lunch.

In the same way that you can't be surprised if your mental health falls apart when you haven't been taking care of it, you can't be surprised if your community, your company or your government are falling apart when all you've done to care for them is shout your complaints and indignation on social media as a way to signal to your in-group that you have the right opinions, just like them.

It's fine if you have judgements. They happen. But what matters are your actions.

How can you push into the fear and uncertainty around you and help your community to not react to those with controlling compulsions like racism, sexism, xenophobia, homophobia, transphobia or any other type of bigotry? How can you instead create an inclusive, equitable community through your collaborative actions?

On project teams at school or at work, how can you help people stick to values instead of falling back into the same old habits when they get anxious working up that Unhappiness Curve?

How can you help the organisations you're part of to not react to anxiety with decisions that provide short-term relief at the long-term expense of the organisation's health and well-being? How can you help your organisation to go beyond a self-centred focus to support its community or the environment?

You're not going to wait until you end up in a hospital psychiatric unit to start taking care of your mental health, so why wait until your water is contaminated and undrinkable to start caring for the environment? What proactive actions can you take to maintain and improve our natural environment?

Critically examine your beliefs, judgements and desires connected to systems beyond you. Are your beliefs helping you? Are they helping your community? Maybe you're wrong about some people or some issues. Maybe you're putting your time and energy into things that won't actually lead to the outcomes you want to see.

And how are you going to interact with your community around mental health issues? Will you try to hide the challenges you've had with your brain because you're afraid of what people might think?

THE FEAR OF STIGMA IS LIKE ANY OTHER FEAR

With all of the changes we've explored in this book, people are going to notice that you're doing things differently. You won't be walking around with a litre of hand-sanitiser in your purse. You'll speak up in situations when you would've stayed quiet in the past. You might say 'no' more often. Maybe you'll stop being that friend who always cancels at the last minute. You'll be able to handle emotions better so you won't lash out abusively at people. You can tell your date you like them without waiting three days to send an indifferent, passive-aggressive message because you're afraid of coming on too strong. You'll be interacting with new people and old friends in new ways. There might be some relationships that aren't part of your life anymore.

People will either ask about what's happening or you'll want to talk to them about these changes because they're affected by them. So here are two things to consider that I've learned from talking about my brain:

1. **If you react to the fear of stigma, expect it to lead to the same natural consequences you'd experience by reacting to any fear: more anxiety, more fear, lots of uncertainty, a shrinking life.** There are situations with very real consequences to speaking openly about mental health struggles. In those situations, you need to decide between those consequences and the consequences you'll experience by remaining silent. It's alarming that people can lose their jobs, be ostracised or shamed for speaking honestly about common experiences that so many others around them are struggling with silently in shame. That's one of the reasons why those who can speak openly need to engage with making healthy changes throughout their communities, at work or in public policy. You can't have great mental health if you're reacting to the fear of speaking openly about your mental health, so we need to make that possible for everybody, everywhere.

    Having said that . . .

2. **Talk about mental health in the same way you talk about physical fitness.** When you get an urge to avoid a friend's event because of anxiety but you go and you support your friend, you're exercising. It's like going for a run or lifting weights. When you commit to experiencing more uncertainty in a relationship and you take simple steps each day to build a healthy

relationship, that's like somebody who starts working on the skills to compete in their first triathlon several months from now. You're building your health. It's not about illness.

Talk about where you're going and what you're building. As we discussed in the Introduction, if you're going to the gym to build strength, you don't label yourself as having a Weakness Disorder. You've recognised challenges you have with emotions and you're developing the skills and abilities to handle those emotions while doing things you love. That is the most awesomely wonderful thing imaginable. Talk about that. Engage people around doing what you love. They can join you in building health for yourself and for your community.

BRAINS ARE CHRONIC

There was a time when physical exercise was only something that soldiers, sick people and professional athletes did. Jogging or working out at the gym were highly unusual. If you'd been in any large city in the 1970s and seen a man running down the street in a pair of shorts and a vest, you probably would've assumed he had hopped out of a window and was running away in his underwear from his lover's jealous husband.

Now, all over the world, it's quite common to live near a gym or to pass groups of people out jogging in the morning (if you wake up early enough to see them). You can easily find workout plans online, you can follow along at home to free yoga instructional videos, and you don't have to pay an expensive doctor to exercise with you. You most certainly don't need to sit on a waiting list for nine months before somebody can tell you how to exercise.

We've made physical fitness accessible. We have to do the same with mental health, for everybody, because everybody has a brain and those delicate imagination organs jiggling around in our skulls are chronic.

You'll have mental health as long as you have a brain, just as you'll have physical health as long as you have a body. Your physical health and your mental health will vary but you can take steps to proactively maintain and improve both of them. That practice of caring for your health is a lifestyle, it's a way of living. It's not a magic pill, an app, a device or a mantra. It's a way of doing what you do, wherever you are, wherever you're going.

This won't be the last book you read about mental health. The exercises we've covered won't be the last exercises you learn. But I hope this is the beginning of a journey for you, a journey of many steps, as you push into difficult experiences, building your emotional fitness level, moving in the direction of your values, up and over many challenges along the way. As you take those steps, remember to breathe. If you stumble off the path on your journey, breathe. In the present, you can always take a step aligned with your values. That next step is the one that matters. The step you take now. In what direction will you step? Where are you going?

WHERE ARE YOU GOING?

NOTES

1 Van Der Helm, E., et al. 'REM Sleep Depotentiates Amygdala Activity to Previous Emotional Experiences'. *Current Biology* 21, 23 (2011): 2029–32.
2 Yeomans, D., et al. 'Resolution and Remission in Schizophrenia: Getting Well and Staying Well'. *Advances in Psychiatric Treatment* 16, 2 (2010): 86–95.
3 Zanarini, Mary C., et al. 'Attainment and Stability of Sustained Symptomatic Remission and Recovery among Patients with Borderline Personality Disorder and Axis II Comparison Subjects: A 16-Year Prospective Follow-up Study'. *American Journal of Psychiatry* 169, 5 (2012): 476–83.
4 Herzog, David B., et al. 'Recovery and Relapse in Anorexia and Bulimia Nervosa: A 7.5-Year Follow-up Study'. *Journal of the American Academy of Child & Adolescent Psychiatry* 38, 7 (1999): 829–37.
5 Hardeveld, F., et al. 'Recurrence of Major Depressive Disorder and its Predictors in the General Population: Results from The Netherlands Mental Health Survey and Incidence Study (NEMESIS)'. *Psychological Medicine* 43, 1 (2013): 39–48. doi: 10.1017/S0033291712002395.
6 Dawson, D. A., et al. 'Recovery From DSM-IV Alcohol Dependence: United States, 2001–2002'. *Addiction* 100 (2005): 281–92. doi:10.1111/j.1360
7 Szalavitz, Maia. 'Q&A: Jon Kabat-Zinn Talks About Bringing Mindfulness Meditation to Medicine'. *Time*, Jan. 11, 2012.
8 Hölzel, Britta K., et al. 'Mindfulness Practice Leads to Increases in Regional Brain Gray Matter Density'. *Psychiatry Research: Neuroimaging* 191, 1 (2011): 36–43. doi:10.1016/j.pscychresns.2010.08.006.
9 Lazar, Sara W., et al. 'Meditation Experience is Associated with Increased Cortical Thickness'. *NeuroReport* 16, 17 (2005): 1893–7. doi:10.1097/01.wnr.0000186598.66243.19.
10 Ortner, Catherine N. M., et al. 'Mindfulness Meditation and Reduced Emotional Interference on a Cognitive Task'. *Motivation and Emotion* 31, 4 (2007): 271–83. doi:10.1007/s11031-007-9076-7.

11 Mrazek, M. D., et al. 'Mindfulness Training Improves Working Memory Capacity and GRE Performance While Reducing Mind Wandering'. *Psychological Science* 24, 5 (2013): 776–81. doi:10.1177/0956797612459659.
12 Biswas, A., et al. 'Sedentary Time and Its Association With Risk for Disease Incidence, Mortality, and Hospitalization in Adults'. *Annals of Internal Medicine* 162, 2 (2015): 123. doi:10.7326/m14-1651.
13 Hayes, Steven C., et al. *Acceptance and Commitment Therapy: An Experiential Approach to Behavior Change*. New York: Guilford, 1999. P. 246.
14 *Diagnostic and Statistical Manual of Mental Disorders: DSM-5*. Washington, DC: American Psychiatric Association, 2013. P. 237.
15 Kafka, Franz, *The Trial*, trans. Willa Muir and Edwin Muir. New York: Schocken Books, 1995. P 213.
16 Hayes, Steven C. and Smith, Spencer –'What Are Values?' in *Get out of Your Mind & into Your Life: The New Acceptance & Commitment Therapy*. Oakland, CA: New Harbinger Publications, 2005. P. 153.
17 Harris, Russ, 'Demons on the Boat' in *The Happiness Trap: How to Stop Struggling and Start Living*. Boston: Trumpeter, 2008. P. 76.
18 Center for Behavioral Health Statistics and Quality, *Behavioral Health Trends in the United States: Results from the 2014 National Survey on Drug Use and Health*. HHS Publication No. SMA 15-4927, NSDUH Series H-50, 2015.
19 Kessler, Ronald C., et al. 'Lifetime Prevalence and Age-of-Onset Distributions of DSM-IV Disorders in the National Comorbidity Survey Replication'. *Archives of General Psychiatry* 62, 6 (2005): 593. doi:10.1001/archpsyc.62.6.593.
20 Barlow, David H. *Anxiety and Its Disorders: The Nature and Treatment of Anxiety and Panic*. New York: Guilford Press, 1988. P. 240.
21 Hanh, Thich Nhat. *You Are Here: Discovering the Magic of the Present Moment*. Trans. Sherab Chödzin Kohn. Boston, MA: Shambhala, 2009. P. 99.

INDEX

Acceptance and Commitment Therapy (ACT) 93–5, 145, 150
actions, changing 77–87
   and coping, checking and controlling 82–3
      checking 82–3
      controlling 83
      coping 82
   exercise: the hierarchy 84–7
   and simple thinking and behaving patterns 79–81
addict maths 176–8
Alcohol Use Disorder 80
American Psychiatric Association 117
Autodesk 66

bad flow, breaking out of 187–8
Borderline Personality Disorder (BPD), recovery from 12
brain (*see also* Everybody has a Brain online community):
   anxiety as 'indigestion' of 145
   and avoiding difficult experiences 97
   believing contents of 201
   and checking 82–3, 111, 113
   chronic nature of 248–9
   and coping behaviours 82
   feedback loops in 116
   grey-matter density in 53
   intrusive thoughts or images from 138–9
   latching on to compulsive fears 129
   and mindfulness 43
   and self-trust 190–2
   trying to help 116, 128–9

cardiovascular health, and raised heart rate 7
checking, stopping 111–24
   and compulsions that don't bother me 117–18
   by eliminating a checking compulsion 118–21
      acceptance and presence 119
      accepting consequences 120–1
      direction aligned with values 121
      sitting with question 120
      taking action 121
   exercise: checking challenges 123–4
   if compulsions not bothering me 117–18
   and from pleasure to pain, into bottomless pit 116
   and totally logical progression of a mental illness 113–15
   and trusting mindfulness practice 122
chemical imbalance 2
clothes and grooming 160–1
Cognitive Behavioural Therapy (CBT) 126
cognitive defusion 94, 138, 145, 148
complex controlling compulsions 137 (*see also* compulsions; Step 11: stopping controlling)

compulsion journey 98–101
compulsions 30–1 (*see also* Obsessive Compulsive Disorder; Step 2: recognising problems)
   addiction to, breaking 33–4
   controlling, complex 137
   controlling, practice of eliminating 135–7
   described 30–1
   eliminating 34, 135–7
     and physical discomfort 144
   fears at roots of 128–9
   and stopping checking 111–24
     by eliminating a checking compulsion 118–21
     and from pleasure to pain, into bottomless pit 116
     and totally logical progression of a mental illness 113–15
     trusting mindfulness practice 122
   those that don't bother me 117–18
controlling behaviour, nature of 134–5
controlling, stopping 133–41 (*see also under* Step 6: changing actions)
   and complex controlling compulsions 137
   and eliminating a controlling compulsion 135–7
     acceptance and presence 135–6
     choosing direction aligned with values 136
     taking action 136–7
   exercise: practising possibility 138–41
     and accepting consequences 141
   and nature of controlling behaviour 134–5
coping, stopping 89–101
   and Acceptance and Commitment Therapy (ACT) 93–5
   and anxiety, stress, depression 92–3
   and coping behaviours compared 91–2

   and coping explained 90–1
   exercise: taking a compulsion journey 98–101
   practice of 95–8
     acceptance and presence 96
     choosing direction aligned with values 96
     taking action 97
CrossFit YKV 8
curiosity, as substitute for judgement 204

emotional fitness 9–12
   and breath 11
   definition of 7
   and exercise 10
   and food 10
   and mindfulness 39
   not approaching as a practice 60–1
   and peer support 9
   and recovery-focused therapist 11–12
   and sleep 10–11
empowerment 12
Endurance Disorder 2
Everybody has a Brain online community 146
everyday mindfulness 46–50 (*see also* mindfulness)
   mindful cooking 49–50
   mindful listening 48
   mindful mobility 47–8
   mindful seeing 49
exercises:
   annoying kids in the car 150–2
   and desires 194
   the awesome schedule 108–9
   burpees 8–9
   catching an urge 13–15
   checking challenges 123–4
   creative human goals 24–6
   everyday mindfulness 46–50
     mindful cooking 49–50
     mindful listening 48
     mindful mobility 47–8
     mindful seeing 49
   the five whys 129–31

healing the inner child 226–9
the hierarchy 84–7
the inventories 34–7
   ideal 36–7
loving kindness meditation 217–20
making your beliefs visible 195–7
meditation 62–3
non-judgement, practice 206–8
   the distracted worker 207–8
   the walk 207
   the wrong opinions 207
practise not feeling right 180–3
practising possibility 138–41
   and accepting consequences 141
setting values 72–3
the switch list 167–9
taking a compulsion journey 98–101
what's on your path? 238–40
Exposure and Response Prevention (ERP), therapy 66

fears:
   of being poisoned 126–8
   driving dangerously away from 69–72
   switching fuel for life from, to values 155–69
      and everything as mental health 156–63 (see also Step 13: switching fuel from fear to values)
      exercise: the switch list 167–9
   understanding 125–31
      and Cognitive Behavioural Therapy (CBT) 126
      and helpful brain 128–9

Generalised Anxiety Disorder (GAD) 5, 117
Get Out of Your Mind and Into Your Life (Hayes) 150
goals:
   creative, exercise for 24–6
   establishing 23–4
   and meditation 58
grooming and clothes 160–1

The Happiness Trap (Harris) 150
Harris, Russ 150
Hayes, Steven 93–4, 150
Headspace app 55–6

'if x then y' thinking 103–10, 149, 162
   and acceptance: 'if x then x' 107
   in action, with examples 104–5
   exercise: the awesome schedule 108–9
   and magical thinking 105–7
   and self-esteem 107–9
inventories 34–7
   exercises 34–7
   ideal 36–7

Jinich, Ronit 53, 56, 166–7

Kabat-Zinn, John 40, 41, 55
Kafka, Franz 133

logical progression of a mental illness 113–15 (see also Step 9: stopping checking)

magical thinking 105–7
meditation 51–63 (see also mindfulness; Step 4: meditation)
   acknowledging limits 55–6
   and addict maths 176 (see also addict maths)
   barriers to:
      mental health and emotional fitness, wrong approach to 59–60
      trying not to feel or think 60
      trying to relieve symptoms instead of tackling problems 60
   being kind to self 56
   connecting with others 57
   difficulty of 51–2, 54
   exercise 62–3
   expecting unexpected 56
   exploring the practice 57
   as human practice 52–3
   for loving kindness 217–20

meditation – *continued*
  modifying, to fit context 57–8
  perception of failure of 58–61
  and racing thoughts 63
  running analogy with 54–8
  setting goals 58
  starting small 55
  staying consistent 55
  struggling with 54
mental-health patient communities online 94
mental illness (*see also individual conditions*):
  diagnoses of 79–80
  labels for 5
  as mix of factors 21
  never benign 28–9
  and physical pain, parallel with 28–9
  recovery from 12
  relieving symptoms of 28
  and sticking to values 166–7
  totally logical progression of 113–15
  worsening of 28
mindfulness 39–50 (*see also* meditation; Step 3: practising mindfulness)
  and acceptance 40
  and cognitive defusion 145
  and doing and being 45
  exercise: everyday mindfulness 46–50
    mindful cooking 49–50
    mindful listening 48
    mindful mobility 47–8
    mindful seeing 49
  and gaining skills from practice 42–3
  and getting more done 46
  and mindlessness 41–2
  and seven senses, allocating bandwidth for 43–5
  trusting practice of 122
Mindfulness-based Stress Reduction (MBSR) 40, 55
mindlessness 41–2

Nhat Hanh, Thich 53, 204
non-judgement, practising 199–208
  curiosity instead of 204
  exercise: non-judgement practice 206–8
    the distracted worker 207–8
    the walk 207
    the wrong opinions 207
  and misophonia, vomit and pants-wetting 202–3

Obsessive Compulsive Disorder (OCD) 79, 117 (*see also under* Step 2: recognising problems)
  and cleaning 162
  recovery from 12
  symptoms of 4
online mental-health patient communities 94
onsen 93

paranoia 185–6
procrastination 31–3
Puddicombe, Andy 55–6

recovery-focused therapist 11–12

Salzberg, Sharon 56
Seal, Brooke 12
self-esteem 107–9
seven senses, allocating bandwidth for 43–5
Social Anxiety Disorder 79, 117
social media 36, 42, 46, 95, 111, 159–60
Step 1: not being a rock 19–26
  and being human 20–1
  exercise: creative human goals 24–6
  and goals 23–6
Step 2: recognising problems 27–38
  and compulsions 30–1 (*see also* Obsessive Compulsive Disorder)
  breaking addiction to 33–4
  described 30–1
  eliminating 34

Index

varying characteristics of 30
exercise: inventories 34–7
and procrastination 31–3
Step 3: practising mindfulness 39–50
  and doing and being 45
  exercise: everyday mindfulness 46–50
    mindful cooking 49–50
    mindful listening 48
    mindful mobility 47–8
    mindful seeing 49
  and gaining skills from practice 42–3
  and getting more done 46
  and mindlessness 41–2
  and seven senses, allocating bandwidth for 43–5
Step 4: meditation 51–63
  acknowledging limits 55–6
  barriers to:
    mental health and emotional fitness, wrong approach to 59–60
    trying not to feel or think 60
    trying to relieve symptoms instead of tackling problems 61
  being kind to self 56
  connecting with others 57
  difficulty of 51–2, 54
  exercise 62–3
  expecting unexpected 56
  as human practice 52–3
  making time 57
  modifying, to fit context 57–8
  perception of failure of 58–61
  and racing thoughts 63
  running analogy with 54–8
  setting goals 58
  starting small 55
  staying consistent 55
  struggling with 54
Step 5: following values 65–75
  and driving dangerously away from fear 69–72
  exercise: setting values 73–5
  and what matters to you 72–3
Step 6: changing actions 77–87
  and coping, checking and controlling 82–3 (*see also* Step 7: stopping coping; Step 9: stopping checking; Step 11: stopping controlling)
  checking 82–3
  controlling 83
  coping 82
  exercise: the hierarchy 84–7
  and simple thinking and behaving patterns 79–81
Step 7: stopping coping 89–101
  and Acceptance and Commitment Therapy (ACT) 93–5
  and anxiety, stress, depression 92–3
  and coping behaviours compared 91–2
  and coping explained 90–1
  exercise: taking a compulsion journey 98–101
  practice of 95–8
    acceptance and presence 96
    choosing direction aligned with values 96
    taking action 97
Step 8: 'if x then y' thinking 103–10
  and acceptance: 'if x then x' 107
  in action, with examples 104–5
  exercise: the awesome schedule 108–9
  and magical thinking 105–7
  and self-esteem 107–9
Step 9: stopping checking 111–24
  and compulsions that don't bother me 117–18
  by eliminating a checking compulsion 118–21
    acceptance and presence 119
    accepting consequences 120–1
    direction aligned with values 121
    sitting with question 120
    taking action 121
  exercise: checking challenges 123–4
  and from pleasure to pain, into bottomless pit 116

Step 9 – *continued*
   and totally logical progression of a mental illness 113–15
   and trusting mindfulness practice 122
Step 10: understanding fears 125–31
   of being poisoned 126–8
   exercise: the five whys 129–31
   and helpful brain 128–9
Step 11: stopping controlling 133–41 (*see also under* Step 6: changing actions)
   and complex controlling compulsions 137
   and eliminating a controlling compulsion 135–7
     acceptance and presence 135–6
     choosing direction aligned with values 136
     taking action 136–7
   exercise: practising possibility 138–41
   and accepting consequences 141
   and nature of controlling behaviour 134–5
Step 12: taming the monster 143–52
   exercise: annoying kids in the car 150–2
   and desires 194
   and expecting tricks 144
   and ignoring thoughts? 148–9
   and not *being* your monster 145–6
   and thoughts like clouds 146–8
Step 13: switching fuel from fear to values 155–69
   and everything as mental health 156–63
     cleaning 162–3
     clothes and grooming 160–1
     relationships 161
     social media 159–60
     work/school/life balance 158
   exercise: the switch list 167–9
   and not going back to normal 163–4
   and reacting to fear 165–6
   and sticking to values vs mental illness 166–7
Step 14: breaking motivation addiction 171–83
   and addict maths, not getting fooled by 176–8
   exercise: practise not feeling right 180–3
   and getting help and support 179–80
   and keeping success close to you 175–6
   and making change visible, tangible and consequential 173–4
   and motivation as a unicorn fart 171–3
   and reasons not to, thinking up 178–9
Step 15: throwing out unhelpful beliefs and desires 185–97
   and bad flow, breaking out of 187–8
   and beliefs 188–90
   and changing desires 193–4
   and disasters, desires for 192–3
   exercise: making your beliefs visible 195–7
   and showing brain you trust yourself 190–2
Step 16: practising non-judgement 199–208
   and being a bad person 204–6
   curiosity instead of 204
   exercise: practice 206–8
     the distracted worker 207–8
     the walk 207
     the wrong opinions 207
   and misophonia, vomit and pants-wetting 202–3
Step 17: making happiness a practice 209–20
   exercise: loving-kindness meditation 217–20
   and expressing gratitude in any moment 215–17
   and how happiness is tough 214–15
   and Stockholm Syndrome 211–12

and tracking functioning, not feelings 212–14
Step 18: embracing uncertainty 221–30 (*see also* uncertainty)
   and anxiety-inducing activities 223–4
   exercise: healing the inner child 226–9
   and the past 226
   and picking creative battles 224–5
   seeking it out 222
Step 19: planning your wilderness adventure 231–41
   exercise: what's on your path? 238–40
   five barriers:
      1. believing you're a unique and special snowflake 232–3
      2. trying to get understanding 233–4
      3. not dismantling the systems in your life built around your compulsions 234–5
      4. mistaking environmental changes for changes in ability 235
      5. wanting to avoid relapse 236–7
Step 20: keep taking steps 243–9
   and brain, chronic nature of 248–9
   and fear of stigma 246–8
   and going beyond you 245–6
stigma, fear of 246–8 (*see also* Step 20: keep taking steps)
Stockholm Syndrome 211–12
stopping coping 89–101
   and Acceptance and Commitment Therapy (ACT) 93–5
   and anxiety, stress, depression 92–3
   and coping behaviours compared 91–2
   and coping explained 90–1
   exercise: taking a compulsion journey 98–101
   practice of 95–8

   acceptance and presence 96
   choosing direction aligned with values 96
   taking action 97

totally logical progression of a mental illness 113–15 (*see also* Step 9: stopping checking)
The Trial (Kafka) 133
trusting yourself 190–2
   score for 191–2

uncertainty:
   accepting 157, 178, 191, 213
   and compulsion 30
   eliminating 82
   embracing 221–30 (*see also* Step 18: embracing uncertainty)
   and the past 226
   exercise: healing the inner child 226–9
   and feedback loops 116
   and romantic relationships 161
   seeking out 222
   and trust score 191
Unhappiness Curve 66, 68, 144, 150, 151, 188, 212, 246

values:
   following 65–75
      and driving dangerously away from fear 69–72
      exercise: setting values 73–5
      and what matters to you 72–3
   switching fuel for life to, from fear 155–69
   and everything as mental health 156–63 (*see also* Step 13: switching fuel from fear to values)
   exercise: the switch list 167–9

Whittal, Maureen 12, 66
work/school/life balance 158
Wujec, Tom 66, 68, 94, 98, 173, 195

You Are Here (Nhat Hanh) 204